PATROL IN THE DREAMTIME

Colin Macleod was born in Williamstown, Melbourne, in 1934. After leaving school in 1952, intent on becoming a Catholic priest, he was told he did not have the ability to complete the seminary course.

He worked as a clerk at the Williamstown dockyards, did his national service in the navy, and in 1955 became a patrol officer in the Northern Territory. In 1956 he studied at the Australian School of Pacific Administration in Sydney. In the same year he qualified as a pilot. Colin studied law by correspondence through the University of Queensland until he left the Northern Territory in 1958, completing his course at Melbourne University.

He has also been a councillor of the City of South Melbourne, an endorsed Labor candidate in the State elections in 1972, and has held a commission in the RAAF reserve as a squadron leader.

In 1988, he was appointed a judge of the Victorian Accident Compensation Tribunal. When the tribunal was abolished in 1992, his judicial commission was revoked. In 1993, at the age of fifty-nine, he was appointed as a magistrate, which office he enjoys very much.

Colin has two sons from his first marriage, and two from his second. He has no regrets that his ambition to be a celibate priest was nipped in the bud.

PATROL IN THE DREAMTIME

Colin Macleod

Published 1997 by Mandarin
a part of Reed Books Australia
35 Cotham Road, Kew, Victoria 3101
a division of Reed International Books Australia Pty Ltd

Copyright © text and photographs Colin Macleod 1997

All rights reserved. Without limiting the rights under copyright above,
no part of this publication may be
reproduced, stored in or introduced into a retrieval
system or transmitted in any form or by any means
(electronic, mechanical, photocopying, recording or otherwise) without the prior written permission of both the copyright owner and the
publisher.

Typeset by Post Typesetters, Brisbane
Printed and bound in Australia by Australian Print Group

National library of Australia
cataloguing-in-publication data:
Macleod, Colin 1934– .
Patrol in the Dreamtime.

ISBN 1 86330 548 3.

1. Macleod, Colin, 1934– . 2. Aborigines, Australian—Northern Territory—Government relations. 3. Aborigines, Australian—Northern Territory—Social Conditions. 4. Law enforcement—Northern Territory—Biography. 5. Peace officers—Northern Territory—Biography. 6. Northern Territory—History—1945–1965. I. Title.

CONTENTS

Acknowledgements vi
Foreword viii
Map of the Northern Territory x
Introduction 1

Chapter 1   5
Chapter 2   17
Chapter 3   42
Chapter 4   55
Chapter 5   64
Chapter 6   71
Chapter 7   96
Chapter 8   106
Chapter 9   137
Chapter 10 151
Chapter 11 177
Chapter 12 191
Chapter 13 209
Chapter 14 228
Conclusion 233
Appendix 1 239
Appendix 2 245
Index 250

ACKNOWLEDGEMENTS

Life was quite miserable for myself and my family when in December 1992 I had my judicial commission revoked. I went back to the Bar. While rebuilding my practice I began to jot down some of my life experiences. Fate dealt me a cruel blow in one sense then repented by giving me the time to write this book.

Fortunately my labours were made a little easier by the fact that my late mother had kept many of the letters I had written to her. In thanking her I dedicate this book to her memory.

At different times over the years Jerry Long came to Melbourne. Very kindly he read early drafts, saving me from factual errors, and jogged my recollection of events. I thank him for his help. Anyone interested in a scholarly and well-researched book on Northern Territory patrol officers could not do better than read his book *The Go-Betweens* published in 1992 by the North Australian Research Unit, Australian National University.

In 1995 I was holidaying on Bathurst Island and gave the manuscript to Brother Pye. After reading it he was most forceful in his encouragements to have me get it published. On my return to Darwin I took my manuscript to the *Northern Territory News* and was surprised the next week to see my script given more than a satisfactory public airing. This ultimately led to its publication. So I thank Brother Pye for his support.

As I delved further into some reports and a diary I had kept I checked material with Les Penhall, Ted Milliken and Creed

Lovegrove. They were extremely friendly and helpful. Thank you all very much.

My wife Caroline and a friend, Judge Les Ross, put up with my endless chatter about 'the book'. My wife read several drafts and indeed was very helpful. Les Ross went through my diary and marked what he thought were useful entries.

I owe considerable thanks to David Greason for his skillful journalistic assistance. Likewise I am much indebted to Kirsten Alexander for her professional editorial help. My story is so much more readable due to their efforts.

Above all, I cherish the memories I have of the Aboriginals I worked with and befriended over many months in the bush. I really enjoyed their company, and I woud like to think they enjoyed mine. In particular, I have vivid memories of Nipper, Nosepeg, Ali, Hilda and the lovely smile of Agnes.

FOREWORD

Patrol in the Dreamtime might, in years gone by, have had a subtitle: 'How a Willy (Williamstown) boy found himself in the bush'. In 1955, at twenty-one years of age, Colin Macleod was a fairly typical urban Australian. He fell within the description, written with generous understatement in this book: 'Most Australians have little understanding of Aboriginal customs'. The same year he commenced work in the Northern Territory as a cadet patrol officer. *Patrol in the Dreamtime* tells us about his experiences during the next three-and-a-half years.

I knew Colin Macleod quite well in the 1960s and early 1970s. The things I remember best about him are his disarming frankness and his twinkling eyes. So it doesn't surprise me that he has written a story which is remarkable for its authenticity, and is told with good humour and humility. It's an honest account of a young man grappling with complex cross-cultural issues way beyond the experience of 'most Australians'.

Today there is an uneasy, soul-searching debate about the issue of Aboriginal reconciliation. The High Court's Mabo decision of 1992 and the 1996 Wik decision have not in the short-term made it any easier, but they have enhanced the probability of a just and more equitable solution. There's another debate about the integrity of historical writings, which purports to describe the relationship between white and Aboriginal societies since European settlement. *Patrol in the Dreamtime* is a slice of a brief period in that relationship in the 1950s. That was not long ago, and it is not a pretty story.

As Noel Pearson has observed, Aboriginal Australians have never asked white Australians to feel guilty about the past. What is sought is understanding, so the the reconciliation process can be advanced. Not everyone is going to agree with all of Colin Macleod's views, but *Patrol in the Dreamtime* is a significant contribution to a better understanding. It's an historical adventure story, with a poignant and pointed contemporary message. It should be widely read and discussed.

The Hon. John N. Button
Former Member Federal Parliament; Leader of Government in Senate; Industry Minister 1983–1993

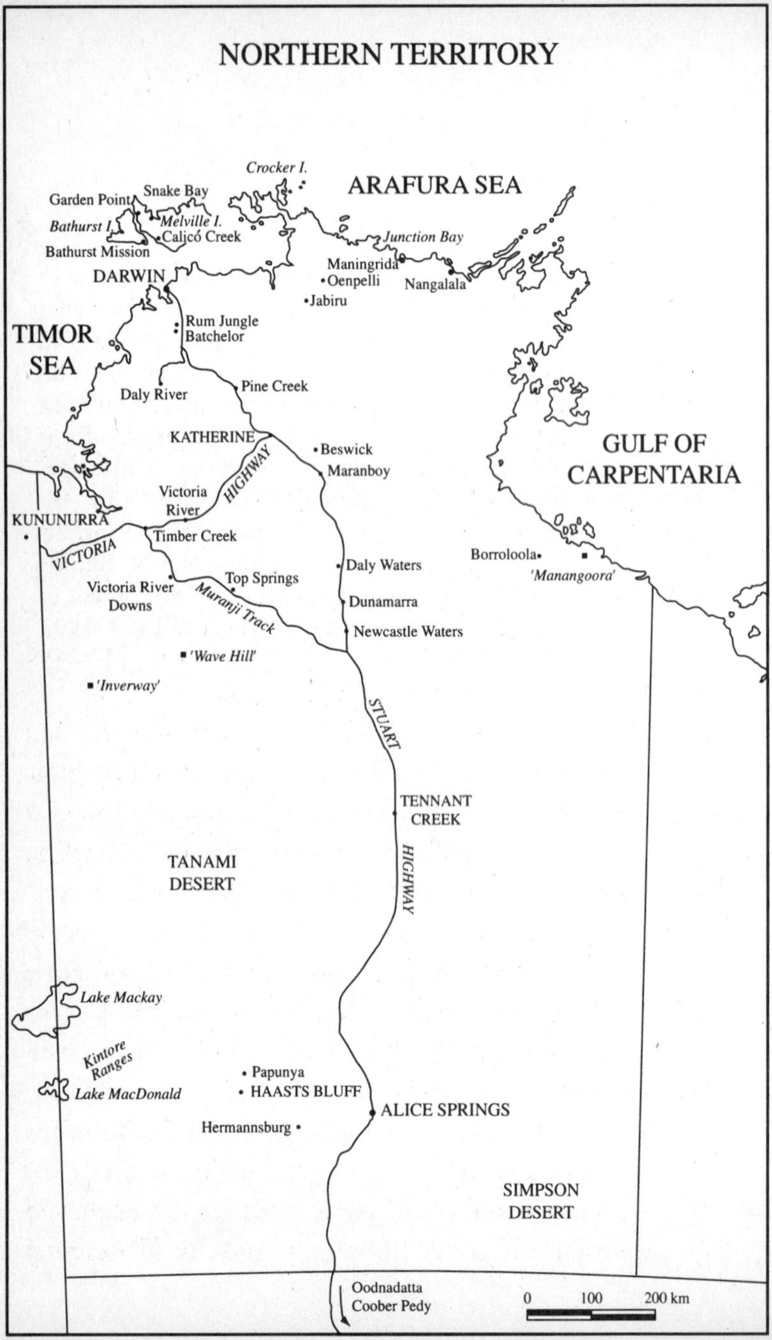
NORTHERN TERRITORY
ARAFURA SEA
Crocker I.
Snake Bay
Garden Point
Melville I.
Bathurst I.
Calico Creek
Bathurst Mission
DARWIN
Junction Bay
Maningrida
Oenpelli
Nangalala
Jabiru
Rum Jungle
Batchelor
TIMOR SEA
Daly River
Pine Creek
KATHERINE
Beswick
Maranboy
GULF OF CARPENTARIA
HIGHWAY
Victoria River
KUNUNURRA
Timber Creek
VICTORIA
Borroloola
'Manangoora'
Daly Waters
Victoria River Downs
Top Springs
Muranji Track
Dunamarra
Newcastle Waters
'Wave Hill'
'Inverway'
STUART
TENNANT CREEK
HIGHWAY
TANAMI DESERT
Lake Mackay
Kintore Ranges
Lake MacDonald
Papunya
HAASTS BLUFF
ALICE SPRINGS
Hermannsburg
SIMPSON DESERT
Oodnadatta
Coober Pedy
0
100
200 km

INTRODUCTION

I first met Albert Namatjira one Saturday evening in 1958 while I was visiting the Aboriginal camps surrounding Alice Springs in my role as town patrol officer. Albert was then Australia's most well-known Aboriginal, whose paintings graced many a home and gallery, whose income for the previous year had been an enviable £6000, and who had even met the Queen.

He was usually surrounded by much of his extended family, but on Saturday evenings he'd be sitting by himself at Morris Soak, a camp just out of town, jabbing at a smoky fire with a stick, perhaps eating a bit of beef he had cooked on the fire and washing it down with a pannikin of cold tea. Despite his success he was a deeply miserable and lonely man, so much in need of someone to talk to that he was willing to pour out his troubles to me, a total stranger less than half his age. I knew even then that this was a rare honour.

His problems were in many ways the problems of his people. He despaired of his own loneliness, but even more so he despaired of the bleak future that he believed lay ahead for his sons, his family and his Aboriginal people. Many times we sat down at one or other of his camps and talked about all manner of things. He was more of a thinker than a talker, and his gaze was often introspective, as if the past was a safer place than the present.

Albert's Aranda people had come under the influence of a well-known Lutheran, Pastor Albrecht of the Hermannsburg mission. In the 1930s a renowned artist, Rex Battarbee, visited the mission, and Albert was seconded to him as a general assistant. Battarbee allowed Albert to have a go with the brush, which was enough for Albert's natural talent to show itself.

It was a mixed blessing; for while this saw Albert feted in a community other than his own, it was a community that made it clear that he would never be fully accepted as one of its members. And the more he was drawn into European social circles the greater were the challenges that were put in his way.

Albert was a full-blood Aboriginal living in close contact with his extended tribal family. In the normal course of events, he would have been registered as a 'Ward', as were nearly all known Aboriginals in those days. Wards could not legally drink alcohol, have sex with anyone except another ward, get married without the permission of the Director of Welfare, travel freely or do any of the things a citizen could do. Aboriginals could be gazetted even if they were university professors or high-fliers, providing they had no entitlement to vote. On the other hand, Aboriginals with no understanding of English, living a traditional tribal life were, if not registered, outside the jurisdiction of the Welfare Ordinance.

Since Albert was famous it would have been politically disastrous to register him as a ward, so Albert was allowed all the rights and privileges of a white citizen – including the right to purchase and drink alcohol. But under white law he could not drink with his friends and relatives. He could not even mix with his relatives without the permission of the Director of Welfare. On the other hand, his own, black law bade him to share what he had with his people. As an honourable man the choice was clear and, sadly, unlawful.

That first night, Albert told me how some of the town's police had blackmailed him into selling them his paintings cheaply. This should have come as no surprise to anyone: the law as it stood for the likes of Albert was a blackmailer's charter. He sold his paintings cheaply; they turned a blind eye to his supposed crime. He wondered how he could escape this situation; I could offer little advice.

Some months later, Albert was charged with supplying liquor and was subsequently jailed. It was a happy moment for some in the local police force, who thought that this honourable, thoroughly decent man needed to be brought down a peg or two.

Albert knew only too well that liquor caused many problems for his people. He often talked about its disastrous impact on members of his own family and social circle, particularly following the brutal murder of a young woman at the hands of a drunken member of his extended clan. But Albert and I knew that liquor was only one small part of the problem for Australia's original inhabitants.

Since moving from Melbourne to the Northern Territory in 1955, I had worked as a patrol officer. For three-and-a-half exciting, challenging and puzzling years I had lived and worked with Aboriginals, registering them as wards and enforcing the Welfare Ordinance that ruled their lives. I saw how we had replaced their independence and identity with paternalism and handouts. I saw how communities could be overwhelmed by 'progress', leaving nothing but wreckage in its wake. I had also seen how 'the Aboriginal people' was a construct by white do-gooders: they were many people and always had been, with their own quarrels, prejudices, and community tensions that long predated white settlement.

I had come to the Northern Territory in search of adventure, and in this I was not disappointed. More than that, though, I had seen good people trying to find their places in a world that was not of their making. And this was the most privileged and awesome sight indeed.

CHAPTER 1

When I left Williamstown Naval Dockyards in 1955, my co-workers presented me with a fountain pen and a sketch. The sketch was entitled Noodle Soup – a play on my less-than-flattering nickname – and gave some indication of how my mates expected I would fare in my new job as a cadet patrol officer in the Northern Territory. I still have the sketch. It shows me, Noodles Macleod, in a well-lit cooking pot, flanked on both sides by natives. One is brandishing a spear and boomerang. The other is holding an axe. I am bound tight with ropes and sweating like a pig.

There were no Aboriginals in Williamstown – certainly none of my acquaintance. Things might have been slightly more cosmopolitan over in Melbourne, but across the bay in Williamstown in the 1950s, even Greeks and Italians were rarities. One of the earliest settlements in the Port Phillip Bay area, Williamstown had traditionally seen itself as a place apart, and many of the families who lived there were like ours: three generations of Anglo-Celts from the same area, with no intention of moving on.

Nor were we taught anything about the original Australians at school. I'd started off at St Mary's, Williamstown, before going up to Assumption College in Kilmore as a boarder in 1943. The only history I learned there was the history of Europe.

I'd been sent to Kilmore because Ken, my dad, was away at the war and Ada, my mum, had gone to live with my grandparents. Rooms were hard to come by at that time, and so boarding school was the answer for me. This might sound extravagant for a working-class family, but dad was on regular pay as a Chief Petty Officer engineer, at the highest pay rate he'd ever been on. Indeed, a fortnight's pay all but paid for a term's fees.

There were three boys: Jack, the eldest, me, and Alan, who was known as Sprog. By the late 1940s, Jack was at Melbourne University studying science, I was at Assumption College in Kilmore, and Sprog was doing his matriculation at Xavier College, in Kew.

In the early 1950s, Jack was a school teacher in country Victoria and Ken was employed as a fitter and turner, and didn't work in Willie. Sometimes he caught the same train home as Sprog. Not that this presented an opportunity for father–son chats before getting home. As a worker, dad travelled second class while Sprog, the private schoolboy, travelled first class. It mustn't have been easy for either of them.

The Jesuits served Sprog well, and he went on to study medicine at Melbourne University. My schooldays, however, were a litany of failure. I first left

Assumption College at the end of 1949, after failing my intermediate year. The next year I took on a job as an office boy in the city but studied for the leaving certificate at night school. I failed in every subject. At the same time I believed I had been called to the priesthood, and so the Church, desperate for new recruits, paid for my return to boarding school at Assumption in 1951 for another attempt at my leaving certificate.

This time I passed, and in 1952 I entered the matriculation year. At the end of this year, all I had to show the Church for its tireless dedication to my vocation were passes in Latin and ancient history. The Bishop was willing to give me another go, and I still felt the call to the priesthood, but I had had enough of boarding school, so I went back to night school once more.

Away from the monastic life of boarding school, the world, the flesh and the devil guaranteed that my piteous attempts at scholarship would end in failure. I was sent off to a psychologist to see if any part of me could be salvaged for the priesthood. After putting me on the inkblots, Dr Catarinich decided that I would find the course at Corpus Christi seminary too difficult. Even then the Church considered persevering with me, until Father Mayne, the wily Jesuit rector of Corpus Christi, declared 'He's not coming to my seminary', and brought to an end my to-ing and fro-ing.

Now I had to earn a living. And that is how I found myself, in 1953, entering the cream fibro portals of the Williamstown Naval Dockyards, known by locals as the

'Iron Lung'. The name was quite apposite. It had, after all, kept hundreds of men alive for years, including my great-grandfather, who had helped build the Alfred graving dock in the 1880s.

The dockyards were at the end of Williamstown's Nelson Place, and my daily trip into work took me past quite a bit of Melbourne's history. The area still boasts convict-built reminders of Victoria's beginnings, such as the bluestone tide gauge and the timeball tower at the tip of Point Gellibrand that aided masters under sail to navigate the Yarra river. Locals can still point out the site where the brutal Captain John Price of Norfolk Island met his end after convicts dashed in his head with rocks and working implements.

After obtaining my leaving certificate, I was made a fully gazetted permanent third division officer, a base grade clerk assured of a life of comfortable boredom. I was a sad failure, in a job I didn't want, in an establishment I didn't understand, for reasons I didn't like. Still, it had provided me with the soft landing from disappointment that only the feather bedding of the public service could offer.

And the dockyards was some feather bed. I started in the filing office, attaching letters to the wrong files, looking for files I had lost or soon would, cracking jokes with my new mates, Lennie, a fourth division assistant clerk, and Swanny, and avoiding the Chief Clerk. Mind you, his ire didn't matter much – as permanent third division officers Swanny and I couldn't be sacked.

It was great walking around the dockyards, boarding the ships and watching the officers in their smart uniforms with the bright gold rings on their sleeves. I could enjoy a career as a naval officer, I thought, kitted out in uniform, and saluted by the navy police as I walked out the gate. There was a lot of time for daydreaming at the Williamstown Naval Dockyards . . .

Life was uncomplicated back then. At six minutes to five the siren would blast freedom for the office workers. These were the days of six o'clock closing for pubs, which meant that after the requisite rushed detour, there would be quite a few wobbly bike rides home. Melbourne was just ten-and-a-half miles away, but hardly anyone I knew bothered to go there. All pleasures were to be found in and around Willie. There was no television then either, so after tea we would listen to the radio or muck about with our friends. This meant going down to the Williamstown Swimming Club and playing table tennis or cards. If the night was a special one, we might even ride our bikes to the local Hoyts or the Empress Picture Theatre, which was better known as the Bug House.

Even so, our tight little group was sensing the first signs of approaching sophistication. My brother Sprog was the cox of the Xavier College crew in the Head of the River boat race. Chooker Fowler, one of Willie's better swimmers, a former Scotch College student and son of the local solicitor, was studying Law. Some of us had joined the Point Lonsdale Surf Club.

By the end of 1953 this sophistication had reached such dizzying heights that some of us had even ventured up to Footscray to the Arama dance hall. The more adventurous among us had even met a few new girls and were tentatively courting. Not me, though. My nine celibate years in a Catholic boarding school had put me way behind in the girl stakes, and I was feeling a bit left out.

Nothing lasts forever, and my sheltered Williamstown existence was about to be opened up. Dad had been in the navy. I worked at the dockyards. So it came as no surprise when the brown envelope came, calling me up for six months National Service in the navy. Odd as it might seem now, I was greatly relieved. I could get away from Williamstown, the routine and the Chief Clerk, and have a piece of the excitement I knew was out there.

The letter directed me to assemble (with a change of clothes and a toothbrush) at HMAS *Lonsdale*, Port Melbourne. I was now Recruit Telegraphist Macleod of the Communications Branch. Very Important. Although I was looking forward to my Nasho, I never imagined that anything would actually be pleasant about life in the Service. But one of the pleasant things about working in the Communications Branch was the women of the Royal Australian Naval Service (WRANS). At work they giggled and we guffawed and they giggled a little more, but it was all for show – they had their hearts set on the Permos, not bloody Nashos.

The women I knew fell into two categories: WRANS and Harpies. To neither group did we ever exhibit gentlemanly manners. Shore leave exposed us to Harpiedom. Apart from church parades and Friday

Divisions we did not get much chance to wear the full bell bottom uniform, or 'round rig', but on shore leave we had to wear the full outfit. There was little that we looked forward to more than playing sailors up in town, as well as in front of our families and friends. Of course, the Permos had told us many intriguing stories of the flesh pots that awaited us.

In Melbourne, parties were organised through the White Ensign Club, where sailors could sleep at reduced rates. For the sailor with an eye for quickie romance, there was also the Trocadero dance hall, across the Yarra River from Flinders Street Station. The tally bands on our caps read RANR (NS) – Royal Australian Naval Reserve (National Service). The girls at the Troc looked puzzled. 'It stands for Royal Australian Naval Research (Nuclear Submarines),' one of my mates said. This worked with a few of the young ones, so we all tried it. But the experienced Harpies knew the score.

Then on Thursday nights down at Flinders, the seasoned veterans would come around the junior mess decks, 'flogging sheilas' in advance of the following week's shore leave. Their sales patter began with them standing on the mess table in auction mode, photos in hand. 'She's a beauty, look at her photo, she'll be in anything. For the lucky one first on, a quid; second on, 17/6; third, ten bob.'

In spite of my virginity (not owned up to, of course), pride dictated that before going ashore I would queue up with all the other hopefuls at the Sick Bay, and get the free issue 'blue light' kit. This consisted of one condom, a couple of tubes of ointment, and a box with instructions in the lid. Ah, romance!

About four or so weeks into the second lot of National Service, the news went around that we were to join the men of aircraft carrier HMAS *Vengeance*, the flagship of the Australian fleet, in Sydney and then sail with them to New Zealand. To us, this was the real thing.

Once we arrived in Sydney, the obvious first destination was Kings Cross. After first getting hamburgers at the Hasty Tasty Cafe at the top of William Street, a drink or two seemed in order. From there we found ourselves in Palmer Street, looking at the girls advertising their wares outside the back doors of dingy houses off the main street.

The most adventurous led; others followed. I followed. I entered my chosen house, and was immediately underwhelmed, first by the dismal surroundings, and second by the shrewish voice directing me to undo my trousers. If that wasn't bad enough, my genitalia was forcibly introduced to a kidney dish sloshing with disinfectant. What the countless beers couldn't manage, the Dettol could. There would be no performance from me that night. All I had for my 17/6 were the memories of a ghastly red bedspread, a kidney dish, and a tart with a shrill voice. I can't even picture the tart. Back outside I couldn't wait to tell everyone in earshot about the fantastic time I'd just had. Best sex I'd ever had, no less.

Next morning all hands were piped to muster on the flight deck and prepare to 'dress ship' for departure for New Zealand. Sydney Heads had not dropped below the horizon before many of us were engulfed by seasickness. No mercy was shown by the petty officers, and no quarter given us by the midshipmen.

Life at sea was exciting, even when we were woken from hammocks at midnight or 4 a.m. with the ship rolling and a cold wind blowing. As a telegraphist my station was the bridge wireless office (BWO). The BWO was very high up on the ship, and moved even more with the ship's motion. Then again, it was said of the *Vengeance* that it was so badly designed it would rock on wet grass.

We were Australia's first line of defence. The masthead flew the pennant of the Flag Officer Commanding Australian Fleet, a Rear Admiral no less. Astern and on the wings were the escorting destroyers. Back home in Australia everyone could sleep safely, with such a powerful aircraft carrier at sea. Which was strange, given that the aeroplane hangar decks were mostly full of officers' cars. There was one plane, stowed in a corner, but it was unusable, only there to show off as a display in New Zealand. There were also a couple of helicopters.

As we approached the coast of New Zealand, a sailor had an attack of appendicitis. On board were many reserve surgeon captains, commanders, and lieutenant-commanders, but none was willing to operate on our sick man. Orders were given to fly the sailor to New Zealand on one of the helicopters. This, of course, meant that officers' cars had to be shifted to allow the removal of the helicopter to the lift. Amid much grumbling this was done, and the chopper took off. In the fuss, not enough fuel had been fed into the helicopter, and a Permo leading hand telegraphist heard over his headphones that it had had to make a forced landing on a beach. Yes, Australia could sleep safely.

After a couple of weeks it was home to Australia. My national service was now almost over. Back at Flinders there was a new intake. But we'd been to sea. We were the superior ones now.

Within a couple of days of my national service ending in 1955, I was back at the dockyards and wondering what on earth I was going to do with my life now. All my friends were moving on in their studies, some at university, others in their trades. With nothing to look forward to, I was feeling left behind, and within a week I had applied for two jobs advertised in the paper.

My first choice was the Fleet Air Arm. Seven weeks on board HMAS *Vengeance* had heightened my envy of the young naval officers I saw around the dockyard. Wouldn't it be great to swagger through the dockyard gates, rigged in a bright new Sub Lieutenant's blue uniform, gold wings embroidered above the gold ring on the sleeves? And although I'd never considered flying before my time on an aircraft carrier, I now saw this as a means of getting some excitement out of life. National service had left me determined to escape the public service. But I was unsuccessful.

The second application, however, was for a position about which I knew absolutely nothing, that of Cadet Patrol Officer in the Northern Territory. The ad sought a young man interested in an outdoors life as a patrol officer and Aboriginal welfare officer. I had no idea what it entailed, but the words 'outdoor life' seemed more attractive than life indoors at the dockyards, and I was raring to have an adventure – of any type – so I applied.

Some weeks later, I was called in for an interview in the old Commonwealth Bank building at the corner of Flinders and Elizabeth streets in Melbourne. The interview panel was made up of a handful of public service mandarins and Ted Evans, the Chief Welfare Officer of the NT Welfare Branch (formerly Native Affairs). I don't think Ted was too impressed with my academic strike rate. Then again the questions asked were not exactly high-flown. Could I carry out rudimentary maintenance on a vehicle? Did I mind sleeping out in the bush? Did I have any questions? 'Yes, what's the weather like up there?' I replied.

A month later I was amazed to read that I had been gazetted in the position of Cadet Patrol Officer. Not only would I be moving to Darwin, this was also a promotion of three to five grades above the base grade, once I had completed my two years as a cadet. It was the only way I'd ever get a promotion, I admitted to myself. And although Darwin hadn't been my first choice, I knew I'd be a fool to knock back such an offer. Nobody I knew had the slightest idea what the job involved, of course, but I was sure it would be more interesting than my present lot. The plane ticket arrived at work a few weeks after that.

Mum and Dad were supportive. Ken didn't know what to make of it, but Ada, keen for her boys to get on, sensed that this might be the break I needed. And she knew I wasn't getting any fulfilment at the dockyards.

The blokes at work, if not envious, certainly considered me lucky to be away from the family doing my own thing. But they were content to lead less adventurous lives, and for a brief, unlikely moment I was a hero. None of them had even been in an aeroplane. Only a few had even been out of the State. They were as bored as I was in their jobs, but I suppose they thought that hitting the grog after work was an easier escape than flying off to Darwin, straight into a blackman's cooking pot.

When I flashed my plane ticket at Crew's Steampacket Hotel on that last Friday night to my mates from Willie and the swimming club I detected a quite different reaction. There was some envy but I think there was also a true pleasure in seeing me finally getting on with my life.

CHAPTER 2

On my last night in Melbourne I lay in bed wondering what was ahead of me. The excitement allayed most fears that I had. Yet two things were certain. I still knew next to nothing about the job. And I knew absolutely nothing about Aboriginals.

I turned twenty-one on July 18, 1955. A couple of weeks later I left town on a typical Melbourne winter's morning – bleak, wet and squally. I handed the Government voucher to the air hostess at the top of the DC3 gangway at Essendon Airport, and turned for one last look at my parents. Mum wasn't crying. Neither was Dad. I think they were thrilled to get rid of me.

The flight was the weekly 'milk run' to Darwin. Essendon to Adelaide. Adelaide to Leigh Creek. Leigh Creek to Coober Pedy. Coober Pedy to Oodnadatta. Oodnadatta to Alice Springs. Alice Springs to Tennant Creek. Tennant Creek to Katherine. Katherine to Darwin. The flight took more than a day, from Saturday morning to early Sunday morning. It was a day of short fuel runs and long stops. At each stop, we'd get out, walk around, look for something to eat or read. There wasn't much else to do.

The closer we were to Darwin, the more fascinating the landscape below became. I was enthralled by the forever extending red plains and dry creek beds of the centre and the hilly bush scattered with the smoke and glare of Aboriginal hunting fires as we neared the top end. Flying at just 3000 feet, we could see quite a deal, even if there wasn't much out there to see.

As I stepped off the plane at Darwin, the heat – even so early in the morning – came as a shock, particularly to one dressed as inappropriately as I was, in jacket and trousers. It was the dry season, and the sky was cloudless.

The airport – a fibro and tin shed – was one of the roughest constructions I had seen away from a beach. Ted Evans was there to drive me into town. There wasn't much conversation between the two of us, which was fine given I was so tired, but it still struck me as offhand. I suspected that Ted was a little disappointed with me. I assumed they hadn't had many applicants for the job, and from comments he had made during the interview, I gathered that he would have far preferred somebody who was academically qualified. Indeed, any qualifications probably would have made him happier than he was with me. On the positive side, though, there was no officiousness in him. Even at the airport, where he seemed to know everyone, he was casually introducing me to people left, right and centre.

We drove off in a khaki Land Rover, which rattled and bounced over the patchy bitumen. Nestled among the scrub was the odd pandanus tree, which intrigued me, but not as much as the ten-foot high mounds of earth. Ted sensed my wonderment. 'They're anthills,' he said, breaking the silence. I wondered how big the ants were. Then I thought of other creatures: spiders, toads, snakes. Spiders I could cope with. Toads, well, they'd be a novelty if I came across them. Snakes were another matter entirely. And I hadn't even considered sand-flies. It was all so new. I was in Australia, but it wasn't the Australia that I knew.

Along the roadside, I saw groups of Aboriginals: some of them sitting in clusters, some of them walking briskly along the red dusty tracks. Some labouring in bare torsos and bare feet, alongside Europeans in white shirts, shorts and long socks. Some of the Aboriginals carried spears. I thought of the Noodle Soup sketch and had to suppress a laugh. I certainly didn't feel in any danger, not with Ted beside me. Many of these spear-carriers waved and smiled as they saw Ted and his vehicle. We waved back and at times Ted would shout a welcome at one of them, as if he were greeting an old friend. Would this be me in a few years time, I wondered.

The bush soon opened to a series of ramshackle wartime buildings and corrugated iron sheds with part louvred walls. Surrounding these rickety structures was a mass of derelict plant and machinery. This was Winnellie, where the 'part-coloureds', those of mixed Asian, Aboriginal and European stock, lived.

After ten minutes we reached what looked to me to be a medium-sized country town. This was Darwin. I'd expected more. On the fringes of the town were simple timber houses on stilts, looking lost in their large, dry gardens. The houses needed paint, and the gardens needed water. Soon we were in Darwin proper. With its streets of single-storey timber shops it looked a cross between a cowboy film and an inner suburb of Melbourne. The streetscape was so stark and monotonous that it lent the fibro buildings an air of substance. But a mining boom was just beginning, and signs of this infant prosperity could be seen in the occasional new building that was more substantial than its neighbours. Otherwise, Darwin in the mid-1950s was much the same as I imagine it had been in the 1930s, Japanese bombs notwithstanding.

Thankfully, there was more to Darwin than its buildings. As Ted and I turned right, out of Smith Street, and right again on the Esplanade, welcoming palm trees and a restful harbour lay on our left. Darwin Harbour was a relief after the miles and miles of red dust that I'd crossed to get here. 'This doesn't look too bad at all,' I thought, as we entered the driveway of the Mitchell Street mess, where the lower graded public servants lived.

If I'd expected a welcoming party and a thorough briefing on my new duties and responsibilities I would have been greatly disappointed. Ted offhandedly introduced me to the mess manager, told me he'd pick me up the next morning for work, and then headed off on a fishing trip he'd had planned for weeks.

So here I was, in a town I didn't know, surrounded by unfamiliar faces, carrying a jacket and trousers wildly out of place in heat soon to hit ninety degrees Fahrenheit. Back at home, Mum had always taught us the comforting qualities of food, so I found my way to the mess dining room. There was naught for my comfort there. The milk was reconstituted powder. The butter was runny. The scrambled eggs were cold. The ceiling fans whirred. There was no one to talk to. Struth. I felt so lonely and miserable.

The bargain basement ambience was reflected in my room. The mess was modern for those days – it wasn't an old tin shack at least. But it *was* basic: a basin with dripping tap, a chest with sticky drawers and a wire bed. The showers and toilets were down the corridor. I began to think I had made the worst mistake of my life. I had found the only place in the world more boring than the files office of the dockyards. I would catch the plane to Melbourne that evening. But first I would sleep for a couple of hours.

However strange and unfriendly this new town might be, any good Catholic knew in those days where to go on a Sunday morning. It wasn't an option, it was an obligation. After my snooze, I ventured out in the unfamiliar heat in search of the Darwin Cathedral, hoping to catch the 11 o'clock mass.

The cathedral was a lovely old timber structure that had been built in the 1920s. The side walls were louvred, the ceilings boasted the Territory's ubiquitous fans, and it was basic, but its simplicity had a charm. At the front, apart from the white congregants, stood and sat about thirty of the blackest people I had ever seen;

men, women and children. If the bare feet in church weren't enough of a surprise, nothing in boarding school or years of church-going could have prepared me for the sight of women baring their breasts in public and feeding children at Mass. I was staggered.

Bishop O'Loughlin intoned the 42nd Psalm, '*Et introibo ad altari Dei*'. The response – '*Ad Deum qui laetificat juventutum meum*' ('To God who gives joy to my youth') – was spoken in Latin by the barefoot Aboriginal altar boy. The surroundings may have been new, but the liturgy was only too familiar, and my enthusiasm came back to me in a rush.

After Mass I struck up a conversation with someone I had seen during 'breakfast' in the mess. Tony was also a fairly new arrival from 'down south', and knew what I was feeling. Together we went for a wander around Darwin, taking in the few sights available. I was surprised to see that the town still bore the scars of war. There were wrecked buildings, and bomb craters on the sites of destroyed oil storage tanks, while from the wharf the masts of ships sunk during the bombing dotted the harbour. Not much work had been done here. Few streets had paving. However, I could now see that the town boasted some very attractive sandstone public buildings, such as the naval headquarters, and the Administrator's residence. Where there were any gardens, vivid green foliage and bright tropical flowers brightened up the otherwise dry landscape.

There were Aboriginals everywhere. Men and women walked around in unbelievably dirty and ragged clothes. Some of them were wearing not much more than loin cloths. Babies were suckling their mothers in the streets. In the main street I saw two men carrying spears. They had very black skins, yet the soles of their feet and the palms of their hands were almost white. How odd. What on earth was I going to be doing with these people? I wondered. And I had better stop staring at them. It's rude.

The temperature was now more than ninety degrees Fahrenheit, and I was sweating. By mid-afternoon, I'd changed into my swimming togs and was heading for the nearest water. A group from the mess walked across the road to a grassed area with palm trees that was on top of a small cliff near the sea. I followed them down a path where there was a most inviting bricked-off sea water swimming pool. The water was surprisingly warm.

I let the plane go without me that evening.

On Monday morning, Ted Evans picked me up from the mess and drove me down to the Welfare Branch office. Any luxuries that the bureaucrats had wangled for our Department clearly went no further than Canberra. Our office consisted of two galvanised sheds, with concrete floors and louvres around each wall from the floor up to about five feet. Mercifully, the ceiling fans whirred throughout the day, bringing some respite from the intense heat. Outside were gardens tended by Aboriginals wearing shorts and nothing else. I smiled, they smiled back, and I wondered what they made of it all.

One of the sheds housed the Director of Welfare, Mr Giese, Ted Evans and the administrative staff. In the other shed, behind a glassed partition, was the District Welfare Officer, Les Penhall.

Les, my direct superior, had been a signaller in the war. He had that easy-going manner for which Australian troops were renowned, and extending his hand, greeted me with the stock welcome: 'We've been looking forward to you coming, Colin. It's good to meet you at last.' I couldn't imagine why anyone would be looking forward to me. I hadn't really gauged that from Ted Evans, then again, I could tell that Les was more easy going.

He had a relaxed manner. Army life had left him with a calm authority, which made people feel comfortable, and the ability to explain situations clearly. He immediately made me feel at ease.

'I'll show you around what passes for our office and then either myself or someone else will take you for a bit of a tour of the native camps,' he continued.

'Ted Egan and Jerry Long are two of our seven patrol officers, but they're out around the town at the moment. Come and meet Babe and Mrs Merlin.' The names sounded like bit players in a Walt Disney cartoon.

Babe Damaso was a part-coloured welfare officer with a soft voice and an easy smile. His white shorts, shirt and socks stood out starkly against his rich skin tones. Mrs Merlin, also a welfare officer, was quite talkative, with a plummy English accent and not at all softly spoken. Their desks were out in the office, on the other side of the shed to Les's glassed corner. Jane Maddock, a lady of about thirty and the de facto of an airforce flight lieutenant, was introduced as our typist. I hadn't contemplated having a typist out here in the middle of nowhere.

Les then took me into the other shed, which was the administration block. Here I was ushered into the Director's office to meet Harry Giese, the head of the Welfare Branch, and one of the most powerful men in the Territory. He seemed very imposing as he rose to greet me from behind his suitably large desk, giving me all the usual first-day banter.

We walked between the office blocks, passing the barefooted and barechested Aboriginal gardener. I didn't give him a second glance, which was unfortunate given that he was one of the few Aboriginal men that most white Australians would have known: Robert Tudawali, who had starred in the film *Jedda*. His acting career had not taken off, and he'd spent his money, and so now he was tending our pandanas, paw paws and bamboo in what passed for our garden.

I sensed that Les was much more at ease away from the big brass, particularly now that he could hear Ted Egan chatting with Babe and Jerry Long. Ted Egan and Jerry Long were both in their early twenties but from radically different backgrounds. Ted hailed from a working-class Christian Brothers school in Melbourne, and like me had no tertiary education. He looked like a strong, fit footballer and he was. Jerry, a very tall lean man, had graduated from Sydney University with an Arts honours degree majoring in anthropology. I didn't even know what that meant. Jerry's father, Gavin Long, had been the official Australian war historian and a man of some influence in Canberra. His son had a similar air of authority. Ted did most of the talking, but if Jerry said anything he was carefully listened to.

I had met blokes like Ted before, but the quiet presence of Jerry was something new. I felt out of my depth beside these two impressive men who were to be my work mates. What a contrast to my former colleagues at the yard, I thought, wondering how I could ever become an equal member of this team.

The Welfare Branch was a division of the Commonwealth Department of Territories. The name gave much away. Its brief was assimilation, and there was to be no distinction between the Aboriginal race and any other races living in Australia. The expectation was that Aboriginals would be turned into Europeans as part of a slow but deliberate process. The very words 'Aboriginal' and 'Native' were anathema, which was why its former title, the Native Affairs Branch, had been dumped by 1955.

Yet if 'equality' was the aim, even the most enthusiastic assimilationist could come up with objections to allowing Aboriginals full legal and civil rights straightaway. Some argued that if Aboriginals owned land individually they would be bought out cheaply by unscrupulous white men. Some argued that Aboriginal people were not capable of looking after their own affairs in a white-run country. So the Northern Territory Welfare Ordinance, established by the Menzies government and administered by the Minister for Territories, Paul Hasluck, effectively transformed full-blood Aboriginals into 'Wards of State', commonly known as 'Wards'. The words Aborigine or Aboriginal did not at any stage appear in the Ordinance. Many people, particularly outside the Welfare Branch, but also many within it, considered the term 'Ward' both contrived and insulting to Aboriginals.

It was legalistic sleight of hand. Almost all full-blooded Aboriginals were to be gazetted in a register that was maintained by staff of the Welfare Branch. The Ordinance provided that all persons gazetted as wards were to come under the custodianship of a Director of Welfare. (Interestingly, the Welfare Ordinance was passed as legislation in 1953 but not proclaimed until May 1957. Between 1953 and 1957 changes were made to the old Aboriginal Ordinance. The Native Affairs Branch became the Welfare Branch, with the Director changing title accordingly. As the new ordinance could not be proclaimed until there was a Register of Wards all our efforts were put into compiling the Register. The words 'half-caste' were struck from the Aboriginal and Licencing ordinances, thus removing the need for half-castes to be licenced to drink alcohol. As patrol officers, we acted under directions issued at the discretion of our superiors, whose powers were pursuant to the Aboriginal Ordinance.) Consequently the Director had very wide powers as to whom he could recommend for gazettal, providing any such nominee had no entitlement to vote, which of course, Aboriginals did not have.

Neither race nor colour could be used as criteria; in theory, gazettal depended on a person's lifestyle. One wonders who the drafters thought they were fooling. Occasionally some people found themselves gazetted by mistake and discovered that, technically at least, they could not legally drink alcohol, have sex with anyone except a fellow ward, get married without the Director's permission, travel freely or do any of the things a full citizen could do. This bizarre piece of legislation would define my work over the next couple of years.

Not that I was to know that. Still no one had told me what my job was going to be. I guessed that I wasn't going to be a desk jockey, but what I'd be doing with the Aboriginals was anyone's guess. It was left to an old-time Territorian and one-time missionary Gordon Sweeney to take me under his wing. Well into his sixties, tall and wiry, softly spoken and always busy, Gordon seemed to be the only man in the Territory who wore long trousers rather than shorts. Physically, perhaps even theologically, he could have been the prototype Salvation Army officer.

Nobody actually told Gordon what to do. He'd consult with Ted Evans from time to time, but Gordon had been there for so long, since before the war, that he just set about his own business. Today, his business was with me. After lunch, Gordon drove me around the native camps near Darwin, and explained to me what my new job was all about: to see to the welfare of the Aboriginals, helping them sort out their own conflicts, and, most importantly, to see they got a fair go from the Europeans.

I wasn't much the wiser from this talk, possibly because I had no idea at all just what Aboriginal Australians wanted or needed. The drive around the camps was an eye-opener. Until the previous day I had never seen an Aboriginal, let alone barefooted semi-clothed people living in homes not much different from those we had made as kids at the back of the Williamstown footy ground or in the dunes at Point Lonsdale.

Invariably there would be a smouldering fire at the centre of the camp, with perhaps half a wallaby sticking out of hardly hot embers, cooking. (Darwin in the 1950s was still close to the bush, so native tucker was never too far away.) There was no way of overlooking the squalor and destitution: mangy dogs, dust everywhere, rubbish strewn across the camp, a couple of sticks slowly smouldering, the yabba yabba of what was to me aimless conversation, women dressed in dirty old cotton frocks, men in loincloths, kids with runny noses, flies in their eyes. There was no running water, no showers, no sewerage. I couldn't believe this was Australia. The conditions were appalling, and the people seemed bewildered. Yet smiling faces were commonplace, if only because Gordon was well known and obviously liked by everyone we met.

By the end of the day, I was none the wiser about how I'd be earning my living, other than wandering around the camps, pointing at dogs, smiling, and stammering in pidgin English. Gordon told me to take it easy. 'Just be natural and friendly and they will respond very quickly,' he said. 'Always be ready to smile.'

He knew only too well how shocked I was at what I'd seen, and how naive I was anyway. 'If they want to touch you, that's okay. If you feel a bit reluctant at first, at least be willing to shake their hands. You'll soon be nursing their babies.' He was right on both counts: I was reluctant, and I'd soon get over it.

The camps were in such a rough state that I'd assumed most of the people were just passing through. But they weren't as itinerant as I'd thought. Many of the people had been 'sitting down' there for quite some time. These tumbledown corrugated iron or bush humpies were their permanent homes. The camps lacked basic facilities but as nomadic people they weren't used to such things anyway.

The men didn't wear much in the way of clothing, just loincloths (nagas); the women generally wore plain cotton dresses, dirty and ragged, and the kids were either naked or wore shorts and t-shirts with a minimum of three holes. This didn't surprise me. I assumed they were primitives, and this is what primitives wore. The church people tried to get them to dress up, but in the dirt and dust of the camps, it was largely a fruitless exercise owing more to fussiness than practicality.

After the disillusionment of the first day, I was surprised how quickly I settled in. The daily camp visits continued to surprise – often shock me – but Darwin itself was an eminently livable town for a young, single male. Each day was likely to bring perfect weather. The dry season in Darwin meant a never-ending succession of cloudless skies, temperatures around ninety Fahrenheit, and gentle breezes wafting in from the Arafura Sea, bringing momentary relief when it was most needed.

Nor was it too long before I accommodated to the mess, its food, organisation and my fellow residents. Most were like me: young, single and on the public payroll. Striking up friendships was easy. From that first week I fell into a pleasurable routine: swimming after work, tennis in the evenings after that as the temperatures fell.

And then there was always the Vic Hotel, Darwin's most important watering hole. The Vic was owned by one of Darwin's Chinese families, the Lims. Charlie, the patriarch's son, ran the place. He was an ever-smiling, rotund and effervescent publican who never poured a beer in silence, but chatted on ceaselessly as he collected your money. Cynics (and Darwin had more than its fair share) commonly said that Charlie mentally added up the profit he made on every glass of beer that he served and that is what made him seem so happy. Hovering around the hotel was the thin, aged and greying Lim patriarch, keeping a watchful eye on everything.

The Vic, with its sandstone facade, stood in the most prominent part of the main shopping centre, opposite the open air picture theatre in Smith Street. It was in many other ways the centrepoint of Darwin. While the various social groups in Darwin had their clubs and pubs, the Vic was for everyone. Well, not exactly everyone. There was never a woman in sight at the Vic. Nor were there any part-coloureds, and certainly no Aboriginals. With the exception of the owners, it was a white man's world, peopled by prospectors, miners in from Rum Jungle, visiting cattlemen, men in from the bush, men from down south with something to hide, wharfies, boat owners and their crews.

The fans whirled in the steamy smoke-laden tropical air. Bare brown arms stretched out from short sleeved shirts and singlets, motioning always for more beer. Loud raucous laughter ripped through the cacophony. It was far rowdier and more boisterous than the pubs in Williamstown, and they had bad enough reputations. Men would come in from the bush – or pretend they'd come in from the bush – and regale the bar with improbable tales. Arguments erupted often enough; particularly if a couple of prospectors had been held up for some gear due to a wharfies' strike not getting the stuff off a ship. It was often said that a ship bound for Darwin should always have its grog loaded at the bottom of the cargo to insure the whole of the cargo would be unloaded.

While Charlie was able to keep order, by a combination of witchcraft and his naturally strong presence, the khaki uniform and Akubras of the NT coppers were nevertheless a comforting sight when they did their town patrol through the Vic. Even my stint in the navy had not prepared me for this. There were no petty officers here – it was man against man. And I fell for it all.

I often missed dinner back at the mess and made do with a hamburger from the caravan in the paddock behind the pub. I didn't want to leave, didn't want to miss a yarn or a fight. And I longed to get my turn at coming back and regaling all and sundry with my exploits.

Many people I had met in the mess were completely ignorant of the lives of the Aboriginals, and were happy to keep it that way. There was such a disparity between the Aboriginal and European ways of life that any social activity between the two races was unlikely. Aboriginals were kept at a distance by the Territory whites. The local picture theatre over the road from the Vic was a graphic example of this. It was an open air theatre in the front half and covered at the back. The 'Abos' came in a side door and sat on the ground down the front. Non-Aboriginals entered through the foyer entrance and took their seats at the back. No one thought that was odd. It was as natural as the two communities' differing tastes in films. When westerns were showing, the front of the theatre was full of yelling patrons. If a British situational drama was playing, the front was empty.

The Top End was at the same time cosmopolitan and caste-ridden. There were anything from 8,000 to 12,000 whites up there, and the numbers were growing as the public service spread its tentacles. Women were heavily outnumbered and overlooked. Social activities were based on men doing things with men: cards, football, swimming. And everyone was socially pigeonholed.

At the top of the ladder were my superiors, the senior mandarins of the public service, together with the professional and executive types. These, I knew from conversations I had heard between Ted Evans and his mates, were usually found in the Darwin Club for drinks after work.

Middle-ranking public servants (the white sock brigade), such as myself, would be found in the various messes, the police barracks, the nurses' quarters at the hospital, or the Vic Hotel. At the Vic, however, we shed our 'uniform'. Any fool standing on ceremony there would be severely ridiculed, or even get his head knocked off.

Within a few days of arriving in Darwin I had discovered the Chinese merchants. As a new starter in the Territory I needed the regulation shorts and long socks. Every shop I entered was run by Chinese, except the newsagency. 'The Chows own the bloody lot,' grumbled one of the Vic's regulars. As a one time aspirant for the priesthood and perhaps a little moved by the idea of giving everyone a fair go, racial antipathy jarred a bit. Yet while I might have been more understanding of their plight than many, I still called Aboriginals 'Abos', and the men I worked alongside were 'my boys'.

Even though these were the days of the White Australia policy, Darwin proved that the colour bar was not as hard and fast in some parts of Australia as in others. I had already come across a few Japanese pearlers that docked at their own wharves. Japanese graves in the cemetery provided evidence that they had been around for some time. Babe Damaso also told me that over the years the Malay trepangers (trepangers are sea slugs regarded as a delicacy in some parts of Asia) had cohabited with Aboriginal women, as had the Chinese, Japanese and Europeans, adding to the Territory's interesting racial mix.

One section of the part-coloured population owned their own homes and were in regular work. Babe Damaso was in this group and I knew from him that they frequented the Parap Hotel and often were members of the Buffaloes Club. Indeed Babe took me there occasionally. This Aboriginal caste tended towards the Europeans.

Another section of the part-coloured community preferred to associate with their full-blood Aboriginal cousins. Many Europeans dismissed these people as 'bloody Boongs' or 'Abos', in the same way they in turn looked down on full-blooded Aborigines. But thanks to the tortuous workings of the Welfare Ordinance, these people were allowed to drink alcohol, a right denied their full-blooded half-brothers and cousins.

Soon after my arrival, one of the Darwin police had shown me how ridiculous and unworkable the law was. He arranged to meet me in a Chinese cafe near the Don Hotel, where the last-mentioned caste of the part-coloured community drank. 'Don't go into the pub alone, though,' he said with typical Darwin pessimism. 'They'll have you and your dough for sure.' I was instead meant to wait for him. Together, he said, we would be quite safe.

That night we ventured into the public bar. I made sure I had brought very little money out with me. No one took any notice of us at first, which was fortunate, as I just avoided slipping on the concrete floor, which was awash with beer. Few women were in the bar that night. As my friend said, 'they would get more than they bargained for'. It sounded like the Vic except far more raucous and dangerous. We didn't stay long as it was clear we were intruding on their patch.

I still knew very little about the workings of the Ordinance, but I did know that full-blood Aboriginals were not allowed alcohol. So what was happening here? Of course, these people weren't Aboriginal according to the Welfare Ordinance. But nor did they enjoy the advantages that the local Europeans enjoyed. They performed the most menial labouring work about the town, sometimes with the few full bloods that had been able to get work, and invariably they received a pay rate far lower than any award. Depending on one's shade of black, a person might stand the risk of being gazetted, so they did everything possible not to be registered.

As we left, my policeman friend said out loud what I had been thinking as I looked from face to face, wondering how to apply the Ordinance in a situation like this. 'The law is a bloody shambles,' he said, sadly shaking his head. 'And you're a mug to be part of the whole stupid set up.'

Not that it was only Europeans who pigeonholed people. In that first week, Gordon stopped some Aboriginals walking along the Bagot Road to ask after another man from the Bagot Settlement. This was the compound that serviced Darwin.

'Him fella bloody Myall, boss,' one man said, dismissively.

Not wanting to show my ignorance, I waited until they had passed, before asking Gordon 'What did he mean by that?'

Gordon explained. 'Myalls are tribal blacks still living in the bush,' he said. 'Some might say they're Aboriginals unused to European ways.'

Many Aboriginals distanced themselves from 'Myalls' just as the part-coloureds distanced themselves from their full-blood cousins. It was clear that anyone with any non-Aboriginal blood contrived as much as possible to distance themselves from their full-Aboriginal brethren in the hope of gaining a more socially acceptable position and in doing so also escape the prohibition on drinking alcohol.

Years later I escorted Pastor (later Sir) Doug Nicholls around Alice Springs. As we were walking around an Aboriginal camp at Jay Creek, an old man of full Aboriginal descent came up and asked who Pastor Doug was. I told him he was an Aboriginal from down south. 'Him not blackfella, boss,' the old man snorted. 'Him yellafella.'

A week or two after settling in, Les Penhall told me that Gordon was going off for a few days, driving some hundreds of miles south-east of Darwin to investigate a flogging – with hobble chains – that an Aboriginal was said to have received from a station head ringer. (Like many of these cases, news came to us via police officers who'd been talking to local Aboriginals.) Les thought I would gain tremendous experience by accompanying Gordon.

This pleased me no end. A trip to the outback so soon! I had never been in the boy scouts, so fair dinkum camping was going to be a new experience. It also meant I got to go to our Departmental store at the Bagot settlement to be equipped with a swag and camping gear. The Aboriginal we were going down to see fell into second place for the moment as I contemplated the thrill of 'going bush.'

That night I was all enthusiasm, telling my policeman mate and anyone else who would listen about my impending trip. I was slightly surprised to learn that few of my new acquaintances had been outside Darwin, and certainly not off the beaten track.

Gordon, myself, and Jimmy Jumabaringa, an Aboriginal tracker, set off in Gordon's Land Rover and cut in to the east off the Stuart Highway between Pine Creek and Katherine. The tracker preferred to stand on the back of the Land Rover for a clearer view and to better enjoy the bush. We were the stupid ones cooped up inside. Often Jimmy would yell out and bang on the roof to let us know he had spotted wallaby or kangaroo. (I couldn't tell the difference – these were the first I had ever seen outside a zoo.) It was very exciting for Jimmy to travel at high speeds and spot so many more animals than he would when hunting on foot.

Before nightfall we stopped at a spot known to my companions. The three of us soon had a fire going with some spuds roasting and meat grilling. Gordon didn't drink alcohol and of course Jimmy wasn't allowed to, so it was black billy tea for three. The night was cooler than in Darwin, and it was with real tiredness and a search for warmth that I crawled into my swag.

My first night ever in my life camped out in the open. No roof, no floor, lots and lots of very bright stars and the smell and glow of our camp fire – fantastic! Nothing had prepared me for being out in the bush, away from everyone and with a cool breeze brushing my face. I looked out from my brand new government issue swag, taking in the new noises, shadows and shapes of the bush that held me in thrall.

The following morning the three of us fussed about as we boiled our billy. The way that Gordon divided the labour eliminated any racial distinction among us. Thanks to him, I saw that black and white people could work together, joke, chat and be good friends.

We rolled our swags and packed our gear before the sun was fully up. I was pleasantly surprised to find that, unlike Darwin, the air was crisp, cool and invigorating. We wanted to get to our destination as early as possible, so we were quickly on our way. I did a fair bit of the driving over the barely graded tracks, finding the first light of 'pickanini daylight' just before dawn, a novel and stimulating experience. After three or so hours we drove up to the station 'big house', as managers' residences were known.

Gordon was a man of few words but much presence. The station manager made us welcome in a perfunctory sort of way then after a little hesitancy led us to the native camp, some quarter of a mile from the house. On the way he yelled out to one of his workers: 'Boy! Might be you gettem that nuisance blackfella crook alonga himfella back.' The messenger went off to find the victim.

The camp was a mess of tumble-down tin shacks, surrounded by people in filthy rags, children with flies stuck to their eyes, women nursing children and packs of sick dogs lying in the dust.

'Are all the camps like this?' I asked Gordon. 'Do any of these people have decent conditions?'

'In the camps, no,' he said. 'The station managers spend as little as they can get away with spending.'

On our approach some of the camp dwellers stood and others quickly disappeared. The smiling faces that I had seen on the Aboriginals around Darwin were not to be seen here. There was much yabba yabba, with everyone talking at once. One or two who knew Gordon and Jimmy pointed to a shy youth slowly standing up from his place in the dust. The manager just stood in his place, his arms folded. If I knew nothing else, I knew he wanted us off his property. We were wasting his valuable time.

We called the young man over and Gordon asked him to take off his shirt. His movements were hesitant and he was obviously in pain. He kept a nervous eye on the manager as he undressed. So did we. By now, the marks on his back had lost the graphic raw detail of the original flogging, but what was left told enough of the horrific story. Gordon photographed the scars. I was horrified. What sort of bugger would treat another person this way? This man had been flogged. In Australia. In 1955. It was scarcely credible. But the wretched victim was here, before my eyes. The head ringer was ultimately charged and convicted by Mr Justice Kriewalt.

On the drive back to Darwin, Gordon assured me that such acts of brutality were now rare. But he then told me of a policeman who, while bringing some alleged native offenders in, found himself without sufficient handcuffs or rope to secure them. So he dug into his tool box and rasped the skin off the soles of their feet. This, Gordon said, had happened only a few years previously.

CHAPTER 3

That trip with Gordon was the full extent of my preliminary training period. From now on, I was on the job. On my return to Darwin I was given the old khaki Land Rover that Ted Evans had first met me with and a single shot .22 rifle. Heady stuff for a young man, but my mission was not as adventurous as one might assume. The weaponry wasn't for protection – I was instead expected to use it to shoot the diseased dogs that infested the native camps.

That was as adventurous as things got in those first days. Not that the job didn't hold its fascinations. In fact, most of my time was spent driving around Darwin with Babe Damaso, visiting camps and workplaces, and trying to sort out the day-to-day problems of the people we met on our rounds. We drove people to hospital when necessary, organised jobs for them, spoke to employers and acted as adjudicators when we saw fights brewing. Even in such 'small' matters I learned more about life than I was ever likely to do dodging work at the dockyards.

Babe was a great source of local knowledge, which meant that he could easily work his way through the maze of local families and their difficult relationships. Softly spoken and always smiling, Babe's gentle way achieved a tremendous amount, and left many more gung-ho welfare officers well behind.

Babe, who was then in his early forties, was very Westernised in dress, speech and mannerisms. He didn't say much but he knew a lot. And like Ted Evans, Babe knew everyone. If you went out to Parap, few people in the part-coloured community, which numbered a few thousand, would pass Babe by without stopping and chatting.

The unfavourable image that some people had of the Welfare Branch took little account of those among us such as Babe, with his genuine personal interest in the people he worked for and with. Even so, his salary was probably the same as mine, which may have ranked him among the highest paid of the Darwin part-coloureds yet was hardly generous, given that he had a wife and family to support.

At first, Babe and I did not do much more than run Aboriginals to work, hospital, or transport terminals. Soon, however, I began to visit camps on my own, once the people there had come to know me. I developed a pessimistic picture of Aboriginal life, largely because my work tended to concentrate on cleaning up supposed problems and breaches of the Aboriginal Ordinance. Inquiries had to be made into the many fights and disturbances that broke out in the camps, and in Darwin. And I had to investigate the illegal supply of liquor to wards, which was often associated with the prostitution of Aboriginal women.

Sometimes a white employer would come around to our office, complaining that a native worker had shot through. We had to look into it, to ensure it wasn't anything more serious than the man or woman having gone to a religious ceremony, which was usually the case. Equally, we had to be certain that the worker hadn't shot through because the employer had behaved badly, which was by no means uncommon. We were responsible for placing Aboriginals in jobs, and our responsibilities didn't end once we'd matched employer with employee.

The work we found for people wasn't too technical, but it was generally decent. Basic painting, gardening, some driving, and station fencing were often available for men, while the women tended to be placed in laundries or big homes, mopping floors or ironing. Dirtier cleaning jobs such as sweeping around garages were commonly allocated. Some of the jobs were rough, although this wasn't always the main factor in workers going walkabout. They weren't city people, and as often as not, the lure of the bush or sick relatives or rituals took them away, and the employers would then be wondering whether it was worth all the trouble. Most times we convinced them that it was.

One of my more depressing duties was the regular Monday morning visit to the police lockup. Here was found the weekend's toll of drinking and fighting: the lot, as the local whites saw it, of being 'just a bloody Abo'.

In the cramped, dirty, smelly unsewered cells at the back of the Darwin police station I came face to face with Aboriginal culture smashed by the merciless tidal wave of European civilisation. The police would go out at night, sweeping through the streets looking for trouble, knowing that they would find it. In the morning the cells would be filled with a couple of dozen wretches – eyes glazed, some bleeding from being in fights, all dressed in rags, bemused, bewildered, nursing hangovers and wounds, lying huddled about the concrete floor over which the toilet bucket had spilled, and on which some had vomited. Almost always they were there because they'd had too much to drink of the whiteman's grog.

Some were unconscious from the night's ordeal, while some lay there, crying to go home. Few could understand why they were there, insisting that they had done nothing wrong, and in their eyes most of them hadn't. Many had been in the cells before. If they were lucky they had employers who were concerned for them: in such cases, the charges were usually dropped. Others, however, were regulars. They were all old before their time.

My first reaction was to blame the police, and it is true that the Darwin force had its fair share of bullies. But they were, in the main, good blokes, working under difficult circumstances – as I was discovering – with few facilities.

When a policeman was a bully or a thug, however, they were the lowest of the low. I remember seeing one junior constable who asked a blackfella to wrap his hands around the bar of the cells, before belting his knuckles with a truncheon. I said 'fair go mate', but I was a young fellow, not too confident with myself, and his glare put me back in my place.

He was later thrown out of the force for abusing an Aboriginal, Maggie Dogface. I saw the incident myself. Maggie was charged with having sex with a whiteman (as she regularly did to obtain liquor). In the muster room of the police station this young cop had taunted her for so long that in sheer desperation she had lifted up her ragged dress and screamed out: 'You wantem look alonga my fanny?' In response, he pulled out a cigarette lighter and tried to set fire to her pubic hair. I didn't try to stop it, much to my shame, but I did tell Ted Evans about what I'd seen. Soon after, the policeman was discharged from the force.

The nauseating revelations at the lock-up were followed by the doleful parade before the magistrate. Even then I could see that the law and the locals had great difficulty developing a fair and just approach to native affairs. The conundrum created by placing a primitive and nomadic people in an unwelcoming and alien urban setting seemed insoluble. For many, it was easy to blame the 'bloody Abos' for not sorting themselves out and becoming 'civilised' Europeans overnight.

The Monday morning 'mention list' was clogged with a medley of wretches, a few kindly disposed employers, welfare officers and the odd churchman. A harassed bench listened to the litany: 'Abo drink liquor, your Worship!', followed by the responses 'Convicted and discharged', or 'Fined 5 shillings', or 'Five weeks in Fannie Bay'.

The courthouse was a replica of our office, another leftover from the war. Concrete floors and galvanised iron roofs didn't provide too imposing a setting. The magistrates court wasn't too formal: lawyers and the magistrate wore shorts. Proceedings were carried out with as much dignity as circumstance allowed. This wasn't much.

There was in Darwin at the time a rather pompous relieving magistrate who became his most enthusiastic when he was seeking clarity amid the fog of pidgin English. In those days the Welfare Ordinance explicitly made it illegal, not only for a non-Aboriginal to be within a certain defined distance of an Aboriginal camp after sundown, but also for wards and non-Aboriginals to have sex with each other, so the opportunities for a grim examination arose frequently.

One Monday there came before the court an airforce corporal charged with supplying liquor to and consorting with Maggie Dogface. She was a most unwilling witness, as she had no wish to upset any future clientele. The khaki-clad police prosecutor had taken her through her lines to his satisfaction, and sat down. His Worship, however, wanted more detail, as always.

'Maggie, you tellem me altogether properly what that fella did alonga you,' he said.

'Well, himfella usem his thing altogether properly alonga me.'

The magistrate pressed on. 'No Maggie, tell me everything.'

'Well boss, he getem his fella properly hard, an stickem allaway longa me altogether properly.'

Still the magistrate was not satisfied. 'No Maggie, you tell me everything that that fella did.'

Almost jumping out of the witness box she yelled: 'Well boss the fella him bloody well fucked me.'

Back in Melbourne, Mum had developed a slightly romantic notion of what my job was all about. She seemed to be taken with the fact that Cadet Patrol Officer and Chief Petty Officer shared the same descriptive initials. When writing to Dad during the war, she'd always written C.P.O. Macleod on the envelope, and saw no reason why she shouldn't continue this tradition with her son, misleading though it was.

Yet however low in the ranks I was, circumstance gave me more authority than I would have had elsewhere in Australia. I soon discovered that I had to develop my own style of doing things. At the dockyards my work had been of a routine clerical nature with no scope for initiative, and to be honest, that drove me mad. Here, however, the decisions were largely mine, for better or worse.

At first I wondered what I'd do if any of the Aboriginals – and perhaps not unreasonably – told me where to get off. I soon realised that these were a people who for quite a few generations had been told to do as they were bloody well told by people who had a huge amount of confidence simply because they were white. We could stride into someone's private space, take command, and know we wouldn't be challenged. And that is exactly what I did, on more than one occasion.

The Welfare Ordinance decreed that all persons gazetted as wards were to be registered under the custodianship of the Director of Welfare and have their names printed in the ever-growing and continually corrected Register of Wards. An extraordinary amount of time and energy was spent collecting and collating names. I could never travel without the register. Whenever I spoke to any group of Aboriginals, I would, if I did not know them, have to check to see if they were in this one-and-a-half inch thick, brown, manilla folder-sized gazette and, if so, ensure such registration was correct. This damn thing was my ever-pressing bible. It not only ruled the lives of about 18,800 Aboriginals, but also half the Territory's public servants. It was referred to by some as the 'stud book'.

A person was registered by having recorded his or her European name, tribal name, language or tribe, skin or sub-section (his or her intra-tribal grouping for marriage purposes in accordance with tribal law), place of birth, approximate age and sex. The scope for error was immense, particularly as nomadic and fringe-dwelling people often changed their names, spoke more than one language, appeared to be of different ages (depending on who was recording the information at the time), and even could, in certain circumstances, be prohibited by tribal law from using his own and other's tribal names.

It was a public document, officially printed, and twice this register went before the Legislative Council to be amended. But the Council failed to co-operate. The people who had copies included our office, various departments, and the law courts. Les Penhall and I were driven mad keeping an up-to-date proposed amended register that never saw the light of day.

I'd often be found bending over the bonnet of a Land Rover, with sweat dripping off the end of my fingers, writing down the above information in a conversation that would go something like this:

'Hello, where all you mob from?'

'Might be some place boss.'

'My name Mr Macleod. What your fella name?'

'Might be 'im Sammy, boss.'

'Sammy, this woman your missus?'

'Altogether properly boss me marry, 'im that one. Might be I marry 'im other one too.'

'All right, you have two missus, Sammy. What their names?'

'No more 'im say that one name boss, but that other missus 'im bin callim Lizzy.'

At this point there would be much laughter from the females, as Sammy had found himself in some dilemma of tribal law taboo, that prohibited him from speaking one of their names at all, or in some cases only allowing me to hear the name – from the woman herself – in a whisper. The woman concerned might then come up and almost inaudibly give her name, taking care not to face certain of her kinsfolk as she did so, lest she also breached some taboo. If I didn't hear it right the first time, then more trouble would be around the corner.

And that was just the beginning. The conversation could then easily have had Sammy giving me two different languages that he was versed in, with the women offering a third. It might have simply been that these languages were all really dialects of one main language, but for gazettal they had to be sorted out. Then we had to determine which 'skin' each of the group belonged to, again with some giving a preferred name according to one dialect and another the same name but with a slight dialectal variation.

The drill was to see if you could identify a person by the descriptions given in the register. Quite frequently this was possible, but often it was not. One often found a set of particulars on a person that almost matched – but not quite. The answer then was to carry on with even more questioning during which time it would usually surface that someone had changed their 'whitefella' name, or perhaps their spouse's name (or their spouse), or a previously recorded age, place of birth, or parent had been recorded wrongly.

Every day, one of us would bring in more information about someone who was already registered, or – much better – someone who had previously slipped through our net. As you can well imagine, the local lawyers had a fruitful time thumbing through the register searching for omissions or errors to get their clients acquitted. As the courts were obliged to interpret the

Ordinance strictly in favour of the accused, incorrect registration created the groundwork for many successful defences. A case I was defending was dismissed after it was discovered that the typist had misspelt the ward's name in the registry: a 'u' instead of an 'i' saw the man walk free. Eventually, the Director of Welfare successfully sought the inclusion of a clause that would reverse the onus of proof, so that the prosecution only needed a certificate signed by the Director certifying that the relevant person was a ward.

Until that time, however, we had to go by the book. The job was difficult, often impossible with dogs barking, kids crying, someone belting a dog, an old man not able to speak any English, with someone else trying to tell you he had two wives in Darwin, but one young one somewhere out in the bush with no 'whitefella' name.

Many of us wrote reports detailing the frustration and miseries of our latest register-inflicted court disaster; but the policy had become the law.

A report I filed in September 1957 encapsulated my frustration.

> District Welfare Officer.
>
> As requested, I submit details of this morning's Police Court.
> Six wards were charged with having drunk liquor contrary to sections 141 and 142 of the

Licensing Ordinance. Of these six, three submitted pleas of guilty and three pleas of not guilty. Those who entered pleas of guilty were immediately fined one pound with ten shillings costs. At this juncture I might mention that contrary to the usual practice (due to the Director's absence) no certificates signed by the Director of Welfare were submitted as prima facie evidence that the defendants were wards. Mr Egan decided that it would be worth trying to bypass the necessity of these certificates by having a welfare officer called as a witness to state on oath that he had searched the Register of Wards and found the defendants' names to be therein.

I was called into the witness box to state on oath that I had found the defendant's name Maggie Nimbali, in the Register of Wards. Mr Dodds, the magistrate, then asked me if I knew this person and I being on oath had to state 'no'. Mr Dodds then suggested that in that case I could not be sure that Maggie Nimbali was the defendant's correct name, thus leaving it unproved that the defendant was a ward. As such, the case was dismissed.

Next followed the case of Dick Lim. This time I was counsel for the defence as Mr Egan could state on oath that he knew Dick Lim. When asked by Mr Dodds if he saw Dick Lim's name in the register Mr Egan said 'yes, but under the name of Dick Lum'. Mr Dodds remarked that whether this was the typist's mistake or not Dick Lim was not on the register and so not a ward.

The report goes on to state other difficulties of the bureaucrat endeavouring to enforce an unenforceable law. In one instance I was the person using the law to prevent a conviction. I objected to a statement of a ward being admitted on the basis that section 82 of the Welfare Ordinance required that:

'A statement or admission alleged to have been made by a ward is not admissible in evidence unless it is shown that the statement or admission was made in the presence and with the consent of his counsel.'

As the instant admission was not so made the case had to be dismissed. I was lost in this maze of white-man's law and I was way out of my depth with Aboriginal customs. The sooner I learned something of both tribal and Australian law the better.

CHAPTER 4

Describing a person for the Register of Wards required identifying and naming their sub-section or 'skin'. The skin system of intra-tribal grouping was basic to Aboriginal marriage laws, and was one of the more important foundation stones upon which their traditional life was based.

Throughout Australia there are hundreds of Aboriginal language groups or tribes. To a degree the terms 'language group' and 'tribe' are synonymous. Most of the tribes, but not all, divided themselves into usually eight or sometimes four subgroups or 'skins'. I have no idea why the term 'skin', is used, but such is the case. These 'skin' groupings were named, had male and female nomenclature, and could be translated within limits into a neighbouring tribe's skin system.

The skin within which a person found himself depended upon his mother. Membership of a particular skin dictated from which other skin a man could seek his wives. Sticking to this ensured that your spouse would be no closer than your second cousin, more particularly your mother's mother's brother's daughter's daughter.

This stopped people marrying too closely to their own blood line.

How the skin system developed is not clear, nor is it entirely consistent with the Aboriginal understanding of the procreation of life, inherent in their 'totemic' rituals and groupings. Here, for example, is the system as it was practised by the peoples living around Borroloola (a town on the Gulf of Carpentaria).

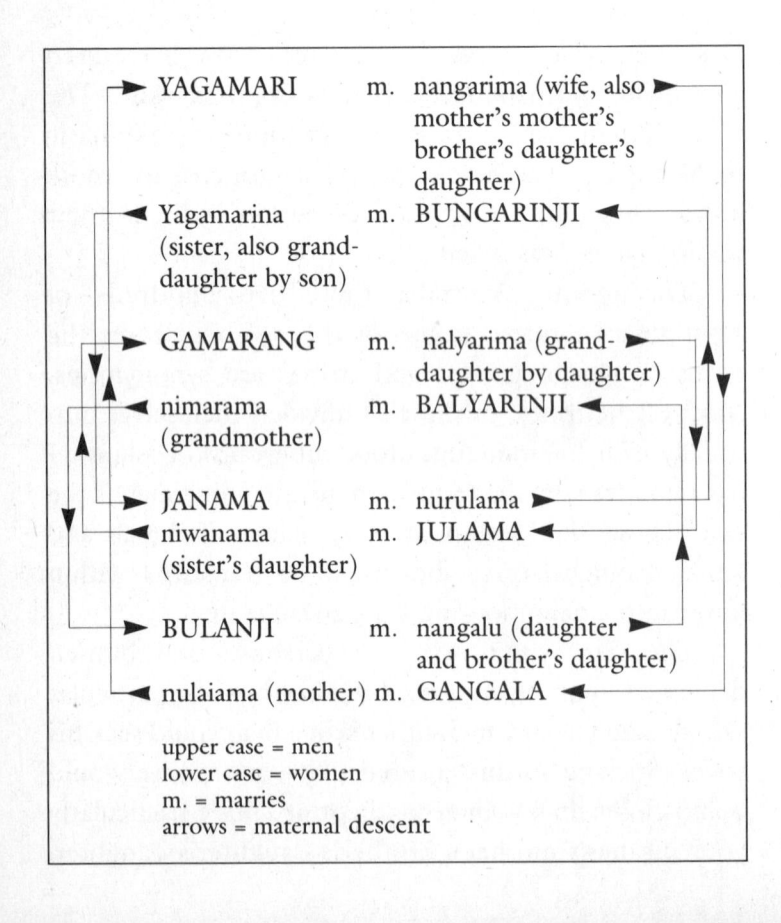

YAGAMARI m. nangarima (wife, also mother's mother's brother's daughter's daughter)

Yagamarina (sister, also granddaughter by son) m. BUNGARINJI

GAMARANG m. nalyarima (granddaughter by daughter)

nimarama (grandmother) m. BALYARINJI

JANAMA m. nurulama

niwanama (sister's daughter) m. JULAMA

BULANJI m. nangalu (daughter and brother's daughter)

nulaiama (mother) m. GANGALA

upper case = men
lower case = women
m. = marries
arrows = maternal descent

At all times the skin passed by the mother. After all, the mother was the one certain relation the new baby had.

So, for example, the child of a Yagamarina woman has to be a Niwanama daughter or a Janama son. And a Yagamari male ought only marry a woman of the Nangarima skin. It would be courting trouble to marry or 'sweetheart' outside that group. The degree of trouble would vary depending upon in which skin he found a partner. If one follows the chart through a Yagamari man one will find that, if all is well, his wife is a Nangarima, his son is a Gangala, his daughter a Nangalu, his mother is a Nulaiama, his grandmother is a Nimarama, his granddaughter by his daughter is a Nalyarima and his granddaughter through his son is the female equivalent of his own skin (a Yagamarina). Ultimately, one ought to marry into a skin in which can be found one's mother's mother's brother's daughter's daughter, or second cousin.

Death would be the only recourse open if relations were had by a Yagamari man with female members of the Yagamarina or Nangalu skin members (where one could find his daughter or sister). Various woundings and minor injuries would be inflicted for lesser breaches.

The female child of a 'proper straight' marriage, for example a Yagamari man with a Nangarima woman, would be a Nangalu. The male child of Nangalu and Bulanji would be a Balyarinji and his wife a Nimarama.

Inter and intra-tribal disputes proliferated among

Aboriginals on town outskirts, away from true tribal influences, where a confluence of tribal groups blurred 'skin' identifications.

The other important grouping was a religious or 'totemic' system of sub-divisions within a tribe. This particular grouping had primarily to do with the procreation of all living animal and human species.

The Aboriginals in their traditional way of life had no form of animal or crop husbandry. Professor A. P. Elkin of the Australian School of Pacific Administration (ASOPA) believed that within the traditional Aboriginal culture there was no knowledge intrinsically bearing upon the sexual transmission of life. Whether this stemmed from not having a knowledge of animal husbandry, or whether not husbanding animals was an effect of such lack of knowledge is unclear.

Nevertheless, the Aboriginals drew a link between the sex act and procreation. Quite obviously the act of sexual intercourse was not always followed by a pregnancy. But clearly the sexual act was connected with the coming into being of a new human life and for that matter of any newborn creature, be it animal or human.

Aboriginals were quite familiar with cutting open bodies of animals to eat. They knew of foetuses growing within the womb. They concluded that intercourse allowed new life to enter the womb and develop into a living human or animal.

Where had that spirit of new life come from? To the traditional Aboriginal, it sprang from the country that the tribe inhabited. New life finds its way from a particular site in a tribe's territory and into a womb of some female in that 'country', coincidentally both when such a spirit was ready to begin its new physical life, and after the womb had been opened and rendered receptive by the act of intercourse.

In the Dreamtime the source of all being, whether animal or human, was planted or seeded in the 'country' by the great dreamtime spirit or serpent. Successively all creatures took their life from the sacred dreaming sites in their country and not from the biological meeting of sperm and ovum.

Given this belief in life's very existence and dependence upon a person's 'country', it becomes obvious why the Aboriginals cling very closely to their country, not merely to have a proprietary right in land, but to bring themselves into being. An Aboriginal has a very special obligation to respect his country.

To a traditional Aboriginal a reference to 'my country', means in effect 'my progenitor'. From this there arose the obligation to respect and acknowledge one's country of origin. Individuals were duty bound to participate in sacred rituals with all others who had that same country or sacred site as their paternal 'progenitor'. All those persons and animals were bonded in a physical and religious sense as brothers and sisters of the one Dreamtime country.

Animals of the same species, say, all kangaroos or all possums, had their source of existence from the same 'dreaming' site. Thus in a given territory all kangaroos, wombats, possums or whatever had their species' origins in a given location within that territory.

Humans differed to the extent they could have sprung from various sites in their tribal lands. Accordingly if a person had his dreaming located in a particular area, say, the kangaroo dreaming, then clearly that person was of the same flesh as the kangaroo species. People were therefore grouped in 'totems', designated in accordance with the country from which they and their kindred animal species had their origins. In a given tribe one totem of people would be, for example, the kangaroo totem and another perhaps the possum totem and so on.

So, if a woman first realised that she was pregnant while in the country of the wallaby, then her infant had entered her womb as a result of that country's life-giving spirit planted there in the Dreamtime. Nothing could be more obvious than that the new life within that woman's womb was thus of one flesh with the wallaby spirit of that country. The child so created was thereafter known to be of the wallaby totem.

All persons, male or female, of the same totem and animal kinship had to insure the continuity of that animal species. Each totem had a very strict duty to perform sacred rituals or corroborees within their totem to ensure that they themselves and the animal species related to them would continue on into the future. The continuity of future generations of animals was thus ensured not by animal husbandry, but by the performance of religious ceremonies re-enacting the movements and chants of the Dreamtime creative serpent that had traversed the whole earth, depositing at various sites the seeds of all future life.

Without doubt such sites were extremely sacred. They not only represented or honoured some god, but were in fact the source of life for an animal species and those human beings who had already and would in the future spring from that country.

Hidden around these holy places were the consecrated objects used in the rituals that the totemic members performed often, but not always, in secret, away, from the other members of the tribe. At times men and women danced and chanted separately from each other, again often in great secrecy from the opposite sex. Very occasionally I was to see such a ceremony. Atmospheric, eerie and evocative. Body language and song enacted age-old stories. Chants, in time with the clack clack clack of the rhythmic corroboree sticks accompanied the pulsating didgeridoo. The thudding of feet stomping in the dust, the darkness of the background bush, the fire, the silhouettes of dancers surrounded by the intense and respectful members of the clan, held in thrall.

Religion, economics and politics were closely interwoven. In the fabric of Aboriginal religion, the Dreamtime, the person's country, and his totem's ritual, all came together in perpetuating life.

Another important principle of tribal custom was that of promising young girls to older men. Most young girls were 'promised' at birth and certainly by the time of puberty. Men were entitled to have several wives. In practice they usually had a wife of about their own age and two or three others of descending ages. This resulted in young men and sometimes mature adults going without a lawful wife.

Having the control over young girls ensured that old men and their old wives, when they lost their hunting prowess, could still maintain control and power. When a girl was still of very tender years she was promised to some old man of appropriate 'skin' to supplement his existing number of wives.

Young men went without a wife until they were themselves considered mature enough. This did not mean they went without sexual pleasures, but it did mean they often had such pleasures either with the permission of the woman's husband or risked the wrath of the tribe by 'sweethearting' illicitly.

The system worked well enough in a true tribal setting, particularly as it allowed the older men and their older wives to command the younger men and women to provide for them in their old age. It had many built-in devices that permitted young men and women to court each other, providing certain taboos and customs were kept. In exchange for the older 'husband' permitting such a liaison he and his older wives were provided with sustenance that their age prevented them from obtaining themselves.

With the break-down of the traditional way of life, and as white culture impinged upon the old men's power, breaches of the Aboriginal law and associated impiety naturally became more frequent. The traditionalists attempted to mete out their normal retribution, feeling justified by their law in doing so. Unfortunately, 'just' though it might have been, such retribution often brought the tribal law into conflict with European law, landing some 'innocent' person in the police cells in Darwin.

CHAPTER 5

It would be naive and crass to suggest that most of the problems facing individual Aboriginals were drink-related, however much this may have been the impression from a visit to the Darwin court. And I must admit that this was the impression I first had, coming into this community with little or no idea of the disaster that had been imposed on Aboriginal culture by my culture. To an outsider, the problems always seem obvious, and the solutions simple.

Many of the problems confronting Aboriginals, in particular the fights that went on between them, often had their source in allegations that someone was in breach of their traditional and cultural duties. The breakdown of belief in traditional values, and the irritation this caused among the older or more traditionally minded Aboriginals, was a significant factor in disputes, and these could not be easily solved by a well-meaning or authoritarian whitefella barging in to 'sort everything out'.

There had always been some generational conflicts within Aboriginal communities, but with the unravelling of Aboriginal cultural life and the allure of Western lifestyles to the young, these conflicts were now significantly worsened. The clash between the young men, attracted to European ways, and the old men, who were clinging to their rights, was often brought to a head in the changed traditional relationships between the sexes, particularly as it affected the rights of older men over younger women.

Liquor and the widespread trade in women for liquor were frequently the cause of trouble between Aboriginals themselves and between Aboriginals and non-Aboriginals. Old men had begun to trade their women for 'grog', young men were deprived of the association with those young women, and the young women were caught in the middle. Only the introduction of liquor into the relationship was a new development – traditionally, older Aboriginal men had unquestionably seen their relationship with younger women as a proprietorial one, and did exchange 'their' women when it suited them.

My diary from 1957 has one such reference:

Talked with old native Captain in an endeavour to talk him out of claiming young Agnes M who was promised to him. He was adamant in his claim but would accept large sum of money. Matter still in abeyance.

Agnes was a teenager who could read, write and speak English well. She should have reasonably expected to take a young man for a husband, and wanted to do so.

Captain, on the other hand, was quite old and had the traditional expectation that a young girl would look after him and do his bidding, living in some native humpy out in the bush on the outskirts of Darwin.

The matter was not in abeyance for long. Ted Evans talked old Captain around to realising that as he was not living out in the bush any longer, but was in fact living with a lot of assistance from the Bagot Stores, it was time to let Agnes go.

A report I filed in December 1957 told a more depressing story. The Litchfields owned a property about ten miles or so out of Darwin, farming an odd assortment of tropical fruit. It was not much more than a market garden. They also ran a struggling dairy farm. Mr Litchfield employed a few Aboriginals – Jumbo, Mary (Jumbo's wife), Jack, and Jumbo's brother, Donkey. At this time a number of other Aboriginals were also 'sitting down' (camping) at Litchfield's, as it often happened that if a property owner had resident native employees, their friends were allowed to camp on the property. This meant that the Litchfields had a source of labour, and the Aboriginals a home away from home.

The natives had congregated in order to perform a mourning and grieving corroboree traditionally celebrated by natives from the Maningrida area of Arnhem Land, at certain times after a person's death. These were the people who had made Litchfields' their Darwin base.

Litchfield's farm was not far from the airstrip and the RAAF base, with its young single men. Jumbo had other wives than Mary, and she, being one of Jumbo's youngest wives, was an easily saleable commodity.

Probably because Jumbo was intent on using her to trade with these men at the RAAF base for grog, Mary was without too much difficulty persuaded to run away with one of the young Maningrida men, named Barney, who had come along for the Gunabippi (corroboree) mourning ritual. This angered Jumbo, who sought the assistance of the other Litchfield natives – England, Harry, Harry's friend Jack, and Jumbo's brother Donkey – to get Mary back from Barney.

Sadly for Jumbo, his friends deserted him in his hour of need, leaving him without any way of retrieving Mary. Jumbo was determined not to lose face and, considering himself a very important employee with a mandate from Mr Litchfield, he ordered everyone off the Litchfield property.

This backfired. Mr Litchfield didn't see it Jumbo's way but instead saw him as the prime trouble-maker and threw him off the property, depriving him of his comfortable home and his position of importance. It was one thing to allow a lot of Aboriginals on your property – it was another thing to be feeding and housing a trouble-maker who caused a lot of fights, and Aboriginal fights could be very frightening with people often seriously hurt. Regular trouble at a station could lead to the withdrawal of native labour.

Jumbo, livid at having lost both a wife and his prestigious job, plotted revenge. With his friend Jack Mukuljuk, Jumbo told the officers of the Welfare

Branch that England, Donkey and Barney had been engaged in 'woman business' (selling their wives to white men for grog).

(The euphemisms 'woman business' and 'women's business' were often used by Aboriginal men to describe many aspects of life where women were either the supposed cause of problems and disputes for men, or the subject of traditional taboos and restrictions. Selling women for grog could be referred to as 'women's business', as could certain traditional totemic rituals performed in secret only by women, such as matters related to childbirth and menstruation.)

Jumbo and Jack Mukuljuk came to my office with their story. When the matter was investigated the true story came out. The resultant backlash saw Jumbo sent packing back to Maningrida. Summary 'justice' was achieved without any need for trial, nor was it subject to any appeal. The powers of the Director of Welfare, bestowed upon him by the Welfare Ordinance, were all that were needed to have Jumbo dispatched. He was a nuisance blackfella, and so was removed. A plane ticket was ordered, which wouldn't have cost the government much as it was the mail plane. He didn't even have a seat – he just sat on the floor. No court case, no appeals.

Jumbo's story is that of the fraying fabric of dreamtime culture. Jumbo, being much older than Mary and Barney, was trying to exert in the modern way some of the power that he would have traditionally exercised over Mary as one of his younger wives, by selling her or allowing her to be used by anyone of his choosing.

In a tribal setting this would have been quite acceptable as the only young men available would have been those whom the tribe and – one hopes – Mary, would have considered suitable. In return, the young man would have provided Jumbo and his older wives with some form of recompense by way of food or other assistance.

However, when the same authority over a younger wife was used by prostituting her to white men for grog, then this was unacceptable to the younger generation. As for white authority, any trading in women was preferably avoided, but on the ground it was felt that some (traditional) situations were more justifiable than others.

Without doubt, Mary was seen even by her own men as not much more than a form of currency that could be used to acquire liquor on an on-going basis. Without justifying such treatment, it had to be seen in the context of a culture where for countless generations, men had proprietary rights over their wives, and could – and did – offer them to other men in exchange for tangible benefits.

On the other hand, white men were more than keen, in a community without many white females, to 'use' Aboriginal women. Much worse, it was no great secret that such women were generally seen as a last resort for sexual gratification by men who otherwise wouldn't even look at Aboriginals in the street, much less show them any act of kindness. This was sexual exploitation of the most basic kind, and to add insult to hypocrisy, many of the whites who took advantage of these women held Aboriginal men in contempt for prostituting their women in the first place. These white men were caught in a self-woven web of self-deception. And, if truth were known, their hypocrisy was also the cultural product of countless generations.

My report also tells much of the relationship between Aboriginals and Europeans in those days. The European names given to the Aboriginals were dehumanising and contemptuous. A glance through the Register of Wards showed names such as Annie Yaws, Pigface Polly, Tommy Oneleg, Bulldog, and any number of labels that could never have been given to a white man. Donkey and Jumbo were names given to adult men. More than a few white Territorians believed that if Aboriginals were human, they were only just so.

Even liberal-minded Europeans lived with assumptions we would today shudder at. I know I was guilty of this. In one letter to my parents, I wrote about working with the local Aboriginals: 'Down at the Banana Plantation, which is usually too far to go down to, we found the gardeners asleep so I got them working. "This sitting on your bums no good, you all bin gettum tucker for nothing." As they are too far away they are given rations to cook at midday. However, I suppose, they went to sleep when I left. You can't really blame them, as it's their nature to do nothing when there is tucker around.'

My nature, on the other hand, was spelled out in the very next sentence. 'On the way back to the house, I had a swim in a cool waterhole.'

CHAPTER 6

'They are a very happy people, but I'm blowed if I know what they're happy about.' Letter to my parents, 1956.

Despite Paul Hasluck's policy of assimilation, backed up by the labyrinthine decrees of the Welfare Ordinance, it was painfully clear that assimilating Aboriginals into the white community was always going to be fraught with difficulties. Aboriginals who had recently arrived in Darwin or Alice Springs from their tribal lands were soon reduced to living miserable lives about the town fringes in depressing shanties. The more we tampered with traditional lifestyles in an attempt to turn Aboriginals into Europeans, the more alienated and displaced they became. Yet we persisted, largely because as welfare officers we could see no alternative. Ideological considerations didn't enter into it – not consciously at least. And it was obvious that if we did nothing we would be giving a free hand to exploitation and cruelty.

In the early 1950s the Menzies Government began running its own settlements. With assimilation still the guiding principle of Aboriginal affairs, it was felt that settlements offering education and schools for the children, supervised work for the adults, and trained medical teams on site could stop tribal Aboriginals from drifting into the towns and to further cultural degradation.

This half-way house system, it was assumed, would gently 'massage' Aboriginals into European culture, by first providing a safe environment that didn't subject them to the sort of shameful experiences that women such as Maggie Dogface had endured in court, or men such as Jumbo up at Litchfields encountered every day.

On paper, at least, the idea was supported by considerable study. The senior educators controlling settlement schools, and the settlement superintendents, recognised the importance of preserving as much traditional custom as possible. At the same time the hope was that they could be introduced to basic European standards of living.

We weren't trying to be do-gooders, instead we hoped to achieve a workable outcome guided in a pragmatic way. As a group of people, the welfare officers represented a broad range of views. There was never any attempt to get us all together to discuss the effectiveness or otherwise of our policies. Policy came from the top, from Canberra, and we had no input. We grumbled from time to time to our superiors but no one thought they had answers, not at our level. We were at the bottom of the pile, and people like Harry Giese at the top told us what to do. Not that I thought we were simply marking time. We were the forerunners for many of the changes that took place in the 1960s, getting better conditions for workers on cattle stations, by making our presence and powers known.

Within the understanding of the time, the settlements certainly appeared to be a general improvement on the missions and stations where many non-tribal Aboriginals were now found. It was true that some churches practised an understanding approach on their missions, but many others did not, and it was the churches – not the Welfare Branch – that engaged in social engineering by removing Aboriginal children from their families for ideological – rather than pragmatic – reasons. Without a doubt some churches, particularly the Methodists, believed that if you could remove the heathens from their culture, dress them in European clothes and give them an education, then they could become good little Christians. They would often send children down south to keep them away from their own culture. Yet they didn't do this out of spite. They thought they were doing the right thing.

Some of the inland missions looked upon us with suspicion. We were their rivals, but we had the upper hand: we could give and take away their funding.

As for cattle stations, regular inspections by patrol officers sought to encourage their managements to adopt a similar approach to that promoted on the new settlements, but much depended on the whim of the managers and the determination of the old men of a tribe, as to how traditional ways could co-exist with the modern. And while the church missions were there to save souls, the stations were there purely and simply to make money.

One government staging house was Beswick Settlement, about 100 kilometres east of Katherine. I had been sent there after about six or seven weeks in Darwin, and as my possessions were few, and my commitments none, upping stumps was no problem. I was given a lift as far as Katherine by a government vehicle heading down 'the track', as the Stuart Highway was known, and met there by the District Welfare Officer, Ron Ryan.

Ron was a portly, comfortable bloke, always dressed in khaki shorts, softly spoken, and willing to help this green cadet. He gave me a general idea of the set-up and of my new duties while we waited for the Superintendent of Beswick Settlement, Alan Pitts, to arrive. Alan had been a patrol officer in New Guinea for many years and had found many of his experiences there an invaluable education for life in the Territory.

Ron took me through the general region of Beswick. These were the lands romanticised in the writings of Mrs Aeneas Gunn, author of *We of the Never Never*, and *The Little Black Princess*. Beswick Settlement opened in 1951, with the intention of discouraging local Aboriginals from converging on Katherine. There were a number of tribes in the area, including the Jauan, Maiali and Rembarrnga tribes. A few of the people had been getting some work at Elsey Station and earlier on at the Maranboy tin mines, but otherwise, work was scarce.

Other smaller groups such as the Ngalkbun from up north, near Mainoru Station, and the Mara from closer to the Stuart Highway, also 'sat down' at Beswick. By the time I arrived there were 300 Aboriginals 'sitting down' at Beswick under Superintendent Pitts. They came to Beswick for the 'tjuga, tileep, plour and backi' (sugar, tea, flour and tobacco).

A difficulty facing Ron was that the tribal life was intact for many of these groups and it was not such an easy task to weld a community out of many different tribes that had been brought together in such artificial circumstances. It was in such circumstances that the Welfare Branch strived for assimilation to erase these troublesome barriers.

Ron and I had a few beers at the old pub opposite the dilapidated railway station while we waited for Alan. If the station was suitably run down, the pub was a bush romance, a true frontier establishment embodying the spirit of the outback like few other buildings could. The corrugated iron walls clung to a sparse wooden frame, which supported unlined ceilings, which were filled with darting geckos. The rattle and hum of the noisy generator out the back, which drove the decrepit fans, competed with the drawling of the pub's patrons. It was, I thought as I gulped my cold beer, a far cry from Melbourne.

In those days there was a narrow gauge railway service from Darwin down to Mataranka. The pub was the watering hole for men who the railway and the Stuart Highway dropped off, stockmen passing through and drovers up from the Muranji track and other stock routes. Sunburnt and weather-beaten faces sweated under well-worn, broad-brimmed and sweat-marked hats. Weary men gathered in small groups about the bar, lazily enjoying a cold beer in a well-earned break from the dust, heat and loneliness of the track .

These were fair dinkum sundowners, clinking about in their stockboots and spurs, holding their drinks or rolling their cigarettes in gnarled, callused hands at the end of brown arms tattooed with 'the barkly rot', a dry and blotchy skin condition caused by a deficiency of vitamins and too much sun. Behind the all-pervading smell of tobacco and grog was another aroma. Men who had been in the bush for prolonged periods without modern toiletries developed a musky aroma of sweat, leather, smoke, dust and horseflesh.

There was none of the hush of a city pub, nothing softly spoken or confidential. Everything here was out in the open and upfront, with no room for bullshit. These blokes lived a hard life and were here for a good drink, and behaved much the same as their cattle would after coming across a bore after two or three dry days.

Alan eventually arrived, a bit the worse for wear, mud-spattered, a little dishevelled and in need of a beer. I immediately sensed I was going to enjoy his company. He was in his early thirties, tanned and fit and though he'd had more than a bit of bother on the road, he could still joke about his troubles in that confident and understated way men of the bush have. Some early rains had held him up, he told us, which had caused him no end of trouble at a 'jump up'. This, he explained to me, was a steep descent and ascent into and out of a creek, which was the sort of problem anyone driving around these parts had to face more than once in a day.

Alan, Ron and I had a couple more drinks and debated whether to stay the night. We decided to get on our way even though there was only the last bit of light remaining. It was essential to put a few extra miles behind us, so we could make it to a wet-weather crossing over the troublesome creek, rather than rely on the 'jump up' that had caused Alan's problems earlier.

You never came into town from a settlement without there being something to pick up and drop off. We offloaded some stores and spare parts for a pump from Ron's vehicle on to Alan's Land Rover and headed off to Beswick along an ungraded bush track that was made all the more difficult because night was coming on. When I had been on the track with Gordon Sweeney a few weeks earlier we had camped before sundown. Contending with slippery tracks, animals and the dusk and sudden nightfall was another experience entirely.

Two or three hours later, much to my relief, we arrived at a modern house that was built on stilts. I'd not known what to expect, and in the outback, it was always best to expect the worst, just so you wouldn't be too disappointed later on. The stores and my gear were unloaded by the 'boys' as the Aboriginals were known, even on government settlements, and Alan and I went inside for a couple of beers and some cold meat served by Hilda, Alan's house girl. My room was comfortable and well-furnished, although by this stage, all I was interested in was the bed. My sleep came easily.

I awoke the next morning to find Hilda leaning over me, cup of tea in hand. Hilda, very much at home in 'whitefella' houses, was a little like the Negro Mammy whose picture could be found on packets of flour in the days before such things were considered racist. I never found out how old she was, but I would guess she was then in her late thirties. Hilda was married to an equally engaging and likeable fellow named Nipper. They had no children of their own but were the guardians of a young teenage girl called Agnes, who assisted Hilda about the house.

Having house girls was novel and, I admit, very convenient. In Darwin I washed my own clothes, made my own bed and tidied my own room. Nor did I expect otherwise. I was soon to discover, however, that out in the bush, whether on church missions, cattle stations or government settlements, all household chores were performed by house girls. On some of the cattle stations, this was a version of slavery; on the better missions and the settlements, this was seen as training for assimilation, and was considered little different from the use of European servants in Australian homes in earlier years.

The range of chores performed here unfortunately included the cooking. Today it was Agnes' turn, which was very unfortunate. On the other hand, we were in no way inclined to linger over our eggs with their leathery yolks, and took the opportunity to get straight down to work.

Beswick Settlement was still being built, and so lacked the new housing for natives that was beginning to appear on some of the other settlements about the Territory. A two-classroom school had been finished the year before, 1954, and this was already being used. Near the school was a large Nissen hut, which was used as a store and office. At one end of the store was a room used as a medical and child welfare centre.

Three houses had been built on the settlement for the European staff. One was for the senior school teacher and his wife; one for the superintendent, the single assistant school teacher, Bill Coburn and me; and the third was being used by a couple of men who were involved in the construction work. The senior school teacher, Doug Allom, was married to a nurse so the schooling and medical needs of Beswick were pretty much under their control.

Alan's main tasks at the time were to plan the building of native housing, contact the natives in the area to let them know of the settlement's existence, and to maintain the Register of Wards. Keeping the peace between the various factions of the 300-odd people based on Beswick also took up a good deal of his time and required not only tact, but also, at times, determination and courage.

To keep the peace effectively, he also needed to monitor those people who were abandoning their strict adherence to tribal culture, but who were not yet sufficiently divorced from their traditions to avoid conflicts with other people from different language groups.

Although my time in Darwin had left me doubting the usefulness of the Register of Wards, I could see that at times such as these, the Register came in handy. Alan often had to settle disputes over some man's rights to a particular woman, and it was here that the Register provided a valuable reference tool to tribal complexities. It was also useful to know whether certain people were absent or were at important corroborees or initiation rituals, as well as for deciding where people should be housed in relation to people of other tribes.

Each morning began with a tour of the camp. Invariably we would find ourselves discussing the usual basics with the locals: matters of hygiene, questions about the number of dogs being kept, registering any new people who had wandered in from the bush some from as far afield as Arnhem Land or from around Elsey, Mainoru or some other station.

With tribal Aboriginals who were still observing their traditional lifestyles, various taboos made communication difficult. For Alan to provide even a minimal service to the people on the settlement, he was obliged to understand as many of the communities' rituals as he could. To know who could use another's name, who could look at who during mourning and who could stand close to someone when certain rituals were taking place, was very important if the settlement system was to work.

In many circumstances it was not even appropriate for a person to use his own name except in a whisper. Among embarrassed giggles, I often found myself leaning very close to a person in order to hear his or her Aboriginal name. For this reason, having a 'whitefella name' was often of real assistance for everyday work as the taboo on names didn't extend to whitefella names.

Rituals sometimes took many days or weeks to complete, and had their high and low points. Such ceremonials required varying degrees of participation coupled with absences from the settlement to permit a person to travel to and remain at the site of his 'dreaming', often many days walk away. Some employers were quite callous in their disregard for such tribal 'bullshit', resulting in consternation in their workers' camps and chaos in their own organisations. Even when we attempted to explain to such employers the financial advantages of having a contented workforce, we were often greeted with snorts of disbelief. Many, however, were understanding and provided transport and food for their people's travel to distant places.

Modern native housing at Beswick was non-existent. Scattered around the settlement was a haphazard assortment of lean to's, humpies and huts constructed with bush timber and bark, cast-off materials such as hessian and rusted iron sheets, and the occasional piece of milled timber.

In those early days of Beswick, it was planned to replace these shacks with a large number of small, simple prefabricated homes. Sites were prepared, fences built and latrines dug. I was often sent to supervise some of the more simple tasks. Developing plans for the future settlement took up a considerable portion of Alan's days and occasionally meant that he had to go into Katherine or even Darwin. When this occurred I was left nominally in charge.

It appeared to me that the mothers of younger children and babies were reasonably keen on attending the school and the health centre. Mrs Allom saw to it that the children showered at the school, and changed into clean clothes before school started. Clothes were provided by the settlement, and cleaned at a communal laundry by women from the camp who had gained experience under the Alloms.

The health centre was always full of smiling and talkative children gulping down reconstituted milk or fruit juice. Yet although they appeared happy, these children regularly suffered from infected ears, and running noses and eyes. Penicillin was commonly administered, but until the children were at school and had the benefit of regular showers they were bound to pick up infections in the camp.

The health clinic and school were often the scene of clusters of women sitting around in dusty circles under shady trees yabbering away in their various dialects. My pidgin English wasn't very good, nor was that of the women not long in from the bush but it was an enjoyable challenge to talk to them. Aboriginals seemed to interchange the letters p and b for the letter f. Finger became binga, finish became binish, flour became plour and so on. Interesting idioms had developed: cash in hand became 'benny longa binga', and when a person died it was often 'dat old man 'im be properly binish'.

While the younger children were looked after at the health clinic, their older brothers and sisters were parading for school. Doug Allom and Bill Coburn lined up the forty or so children in their clean school clothes. To the accompaniment of a scratchy record, grinding out a British marching tune, the ragged but eager flock of young children, fresh from the showers, would strut to the school rooms. The syllabus was basic reading, writing and arithmetic. Attendances were erratic and we could never enforce them, but without any doubt the students were learning to read, write and understand a little of Western ways, while not being discouraged to be proud of their inheritance.

The tools for assimilation were drawn from wherever possible. Beswick had a communal kitchen staffed by trained natives, who prepared one meal a day from rations. 'Their tucker is terrible by our standards but to them it is "number one tucker" as they call it,' I wrote to my mother. 'They only have one hot meal a day and that is stew (eaten with chunks of bread from a shared bowl); the other meals are just bread and jam, but even that is paradise to natives who have just come in from the bush.

'Last week we started a new idea here and gave the school kids dinner together. We got natives to paint a large room and had tables put in it, and had special bread baked and stew cooked and also custard and tinned fruit. The kids had to use a spoon to eat it, the first time in their lives that they have had any plates or cutlery and we made sure they didn't use their fingers.

'So from now on they will eat each midday meal together instead of going down to the camp where the tucker is eaten with fingers and where dogs and pigs and parents get everything. This was the first good meal these kids have had in their lives.'

('Number one tucker', as the natives called their favourite food, took on various forms, as I also told my parents in one 1955 letter. 'Jack talks of snakes, well I have seen quite a few here now. One of them must have been about ten feet long, and the boys pounced on it. "Number one tucker", and by Jove they mean it, even offer me some, but I haven't been game yet. However, the other day I very gingerly tasted a lizard which had been cooked whole on an open fire out in the bush. It had a very sweet flavour, really too sweet for me to eat.')

Mrs Allom's clinic also catered for adults, and if we found someone sick we tried to persuade them to attend. This was not always easy, particularly with the frail and aged, with whom there were also the difficulties of language, and the complexities of taboo. Old men naturally had a reticence to use our medicine when practised by a female.

Beswick camp life with its crowding, squalor, diseased dogs was not the traditional life its inmates were used to. Until better housing was in place it was the only step between their free nomadic existence and assimilation, and it was not a promising step. Whether it provided the answer did not become apparent to me while I was there, but even so, I couldn't see any better approach.

The settlement concept assumed that with grog and exploitation eradicated at the same time as health clinics and schools were being introduced, there was a good chance of assimilation. Camp environments on cattle stations and church missions or the fringe dwelling shanties also had their own pluses and minuses. Most of them lost some quality of life compared to the tribal lifestyle. However, that lifestyle was breaking down and even before then often compared poorly in many aspects with what the European was offering.

Idealists argued that the Aboriginals ought to have been left alone, but that flew in the face of reality. Post-1788, this could only have been implemented by forcibly barring people from the towns and cattle stations. There was no way such apartheid could have been enforced, and the idealists would have been the first to complain.

In any event, the traditional lifestyle was not as marvellous as its promoters and defenders claimed. Idyllic scenes of blissful natives basking in sunshine, content with their lot in life, and surrounded by food at every turn were fraudulent and romantic. The grim reality for many Aboriginals in the Territory was a very harsh climate, infanticide, violence against women, primitive abortion, dying of thirst and 'doing a perish' for days without food. In such circumstances, even the patronising and imperfect setting of a government settlement was preferable to many. And yet . . .

Near Beswick was an abandoned mine, around which a number of prospectors fossicked for tin. These prospectors attracted a gathering of Aboriginal families about them, whom they 'employed' in a very rough and ready way. Part of our job was to keep a check on these characters to ensure that there was no supplying of liquor or trading liquor for women.

This was not as easy as it sounds. The lure of grog, and the willingness of men to trade 'their' women made detection very difficult. Usually we were able to act only if the situation took a nasty turn, say, for example, if some poor 'lubra' appeared at the clinic with a split skull for not doing as she was told – split by her husband, who usually was not a white man. And this happened, quite often. Up at Katherine Hospital, later, while we'd be sorting this mess out, someone would invariably remark how our critics from down south (who resented our interference in 'the natural order') could learn by seeing what sometimes prompted our intervention.

It was obvious that once food could be produced from a tin or flour bag in the whiteman's store, the hold the totemic dances and blood letting rituals of the Dreamtime had over the younger generation would loosen. What was once sacred dogma would soon be merely traditional.

In areas such as Beswick, unlike life for the fringe dwellers around Darwin or Alice Springs, traditional culture still required the attendance of children at some tribal rituals and association with their elders to be taught the ways of their forefathers. This was particularly true for those boys who were reaching the age of puberty, when long absences were required not only for the ceremonies associated with their circumcision, but also for the protracted instruction and isolation when they were inducted into the tribe as young men.

The songs of the Dreamtime, the hiding places of the sacred objects used in rituals (sometimes called churingas), and the stories and law of their skin, totem, and tribe were all very important, even if beliefs were dissipating. I wondered how much longer these rituals would be with us, outside anthropology textbooks, assimilation policy or no assimilation policy.

Night times at Beswick were a little lonely, but as we had a generator for electricity, Bill Coburn, Alan and I could always read and talk, which kept the boredom at bay. In isolated settings where there is not much else to do, men are easily tempted to drink, but Alan had that firmly under control and it was only on the rare occasion that we had a breakout. Almost always such a breakout was associated with the arrival of a visitor, such as old

Jock McKay passing through to or from Katherine from his station, 'Mainoru'.

Jock was one of the Territory's true characters. He was a small wiry man of about five foot four, with a harelip. Jock couldn't care less about decorum, as he lived a fairly lonely life out at Mainoru. He also loved his rum. In the outback of those days with limited refrigeration, Beenleigh Rum was *the* drink, although ex-New Guinea hands like Alan preferred Rhum Negrita. Rum, given the amount of alcohol it packed, took up a lot less room than beer, could be transported more cheaply and be mixed with all sorts of water, whether from muddy creeks, bores, tanks, or soaks in the desert. Few Territorians went outback without this staple ingredient stowed safely in their tucker box.

The wet season was approaching, which meant Jock had to make many last minute desperate trips into Katherine, before the tracks through the bush would be impassable. He became bogged on one of these trips, so he sent his 'boys' on foot into Beswick seeking our aid to help him out. To be on the safe side we took out a tractor and a winch. Alan was cursing Jock as we bounced over the ungraded and muddy track to the scene of Jock's misery.

Turning a corner on the track we came upon a vision of pure bedlam. The wiry little bugger was wielding a shovel and bellowing expletives fifty to the dozen at his boys, who kept well clear. On seeing we had arrived, he directed his anger our way, giving us an earful for our tardiness.

Extricating Jock from the bog was a thankless task. There was no stopping the cascade of instructions and invective. The Aboriginals were not much use as Jock had abused and terrorised them into inertia. The tractor hauled away, Jock spun the wheels into the black sticky earth, and we were mud-spattered and irascible. Only by combining winch, tractor and Alan shouting down Jock was the truck dragged from the mud.

To hear Jock discuss bogs was an experience in itself. He rated them by how much rum he had to knock back to get out of them. His normal approach was to have a bottle for each wheel bogged. This ranged from a 'one bottler' to 'a fuckin' four bottler', although with the hare-lip and rum this came out as 'a 'huckin 'or 'ottler'.

We were soon on our way back to the comfort of Beswick, our anger fading as we contemplated a rewarding rum. We all agreed this ought be at Jock's expense; however, Alan reckoned Beenleigh Rum tasted like kerosene, so we broached his supply of Rhum Negrita. This he had ordered in especially from the New Guinea bar of Ushers Hotel in Sydney. Jock didn't argue with the brand so long as it was rum and we all settled down to listen to Jock's tales of the bush.

After Jock had had a few, Alan got him to tell us the story of Ernestine Hill's visit. The famous author of *The Territory* was a very proper person, despite the rough and ready setting of her books. On one occasion this epitome of feminine correctness was stranded for some days at Mainoru, and was left to the less-than-tender mercies of Jock. During the first evening of her stay, Jock treated Miss Hill to one of his famed dinners of salt beef and tinned vegetables. Naturally, Miss Hill had need to drink a good deal of water to balance out the salt beef. Even a lady such as she had need of a toilet, and finally she plucked up the courage to ask Jock where the same could be had. By this time Jock, having enveloped a goodly quantity of rum, was warming to his visitor. He rose to his feet, opened the door to the starry outback night and said: 'Go 'oo it, 'ady, it's the biggest huckin gin house in orl the huckin world.'

Life was never dull. One morning Doug Allom appeared at the house at what would normally have been school time. 'None of the kids have turned up; there must be a bloody fight on down the camp.' Alan looked at me and suggested that I find clean white shorts, shirt and long socks. I had not worn such pristine pukka clothes since being in Darwin. Hilda always had our clothes spotless and well ironed, so I was soon transformed into something resembling a Darwin civil servant. Alan appeared very quickly decked out in similar gear, and we made our way to the camp, with Alan in the lead telling me to look confident, look to the front and not to hesitate.

Alan was very much a product of New Guinea and its methods, as seen in the white pukka outfit as fight-stopper. By now he had been the mentor I had most time with in the bush, and it was to him I then looked. While I still admire his capacity and enthusiasm, I have since discovered there are many ways to skin a cat.

Others more versed in the ways of the Territory would not have been as colonial in their approach.

Sure enough, when we arrived at the camp there were two men fighting it out with heavy sticks. On either side of them were opposing groups of angry natives shouting and throwing the odd spear in encouragement. I was scared stiff as I followed a step or two behind Alan. He never hesitated but walked straight up to the two men and without a quiver in his voice demanded that each hand over their fighting sticks. To my great surprise – and relief – they did. With that he told them to follow him up to the office. Alan then turned his back upon them, showing he was without fear, and began in a measured and confident way to walk away, presuming they would do his bidding. They followed.

On our arrival at his office he sent a messenger to the camp to have all their property, wives and children sent up. Alan knew a fair bit of the background to the fight, enough to know that it was not a result of some breach of tribal law, but rather the culmination of bad blood that had been brewing for some time between the two men. These two had been troublemakers while working on a cattle station and had disrupted life there. For that reason they had been sent to Beswick, but this had only worsened the aggro between the two.

There was no alternative but to use the harshest penalty we could impose – banishment. To send someone from their country was a punishment we certainly would not have used in the case of someone very much imbued with traditional values. In this case, however, Alan felt the trouble had gone on long enough, and so decreed that separating the two was in the best interests of all.

Later that day, one man and his family were sent to Katherine en route to Darwin, and the other shortly after, by separate vehicle en route to Alice Springs. Such were our powers, that without any reference to a court of law, the two families were sent for six months into country they did not know, to people they did not know, who spoke a language they did not know and where the customs and food were no doubt different from what they knew.

In the main, our power was exercised as humanely as possible and with common sense. As all in question were to be gazetted as wards, the Director of Welfare and his delegates could remove them without recourse to any court, to any place in the Territory. When one thinks about such power today it seems scarcely believable that it could be exercised outside of a dictatorship.

There were no hard feelings in the camp towards us. In a letter home after I described this incident I wrote: 'That night we were invited to a corroboree (one never goes without being invited and taking a gift) and found it most interesting and eerie. A dark, still night with fires and natives all very primitive and in the native setting, doing their dances etc to the music of clapping sticks and a didgeridoo (an instrument with a pulsating sort of sound). They have invited us again tomorrow night to "a really big business boss", which will be a more serious corroboree.'

I'd soon learnt that I couldn't rely on the old assumptions that I'd brought with me from Williamstown to judge the complex situations now facing me. Obviously it was important that I had an understanding of some basic principles of Aboriginal culture. This wasn't just another public service job, as those who administered the Welfare Branch knew. But I had no idea where I would pick up an unbiased overview of Aboriginal folkways.

The other patrol officers were very knowledgeable, sure, but they were without formal training in their field. Even so, we all had responsibilities that desperately needed expertise, and none of us was given any time to get up to speed upon arriving in the Territory – we were all dropped in the thick of it immediately, exercising responsibilities that few men of our age down south would face. Indeed, such were my assumptions about how the system worked that I never actually bothered to ask whether any substantial training was in the pipelines. The Welfare Branch was a rough-and-ready set-up, and to inquire after training seemed a bit soft.

But while at Beswick, confirmation came through that in the following year, 1956, I would be part of the first intake of Northern Territory patrol officers in the ASOPA training course in Sydney. ASOPA, the

Australian School of Pacific Administration, was the successor to the wartime Australian New Guinea Auxiliary Unit (ANGAU), which trained coast watchers and the like. ASOPA was set up to instruct those who were to work in the Territories of Papua and New Guinea.

Five of us were selected to go on the course from the Northern Territory: myself, Jerry Long, Ted Egan, Brian Greenfield and Pat Leonard. The course was to include tuition in anthropology under the guidance of the Emeritus Professor of Anthropology at the University of Sydney, A. P. Elkin. Until then, my training would be strictly on the job. I was quite pleased with myself. Of course, some of my older colleagues – who weren't going – thought it was a load of bullshit. But I knew it would give me the depth I needed if I was to understand my job properly.

Alan, an old boy of ANGAU from his New Guinea days, congratulated me on my good fortune, wished me well and regaled me with the good times he had had there. I already had my memory of a day in Sydney as a national serviceman: the thought of a year of such pleasures was mind-boggling.

After I made my farewells to the Alloms, Hilda and Agnes, Alan and Bill Coburn drove me to Katherine. We had steak and eggs for dinner at the little tin shed cafe then walked along the wooden sidewalk to the pub for a farewell drink.

All three of us stayed the night in the corrugated iron-walled bedrooms, with antiquated beds on concrete floors. Eventually, despite the cacophony of stockmen, fencers and young ringers drinking, singing, and fighting, I fell asleep. The next morning we said our goodbyes, and I hitched a lift on a truck going back to Darwin that Ron Ryan had organised for me.

Darwin had not changed in the couple of months I'd been away, but I certainly had. The time spent at Beswick had in my view put me ahead of the deskbound 'office wallahs'. Many in the Mitchell Street mess had never been further south than the swimming hole at Howard Springs, despite spending years in Darwin. The routine of two months earlier no longer seemed so incomprehensible. Speaking to the natives was now neither novel nor intimidating. My time spent living with Aboriginals in their all but tribal state had given me an insight into Aboriginal Australia that city-dwellers were never likely to achieve. I hoped I hadn't become a know-all in that short time, but I knew that Colin Macleod had crossed a watershed.

CHAPTER 7

My new-found confidence was sorely shaken when I entered ASOPA late in January 1956. Twenty-six students answered the first roll call, twenty-one from Papua and New Guinea and five from the Northern Territory. I was the youngest and by far the most inexperienced of all the students, and I was in very experienced company.

If anything was likely to set my nerves on edge, following my less than spectacular academic record at school, it was studying with grown-ups. Although I was enthusiastic about being here, and marvelled at my luck, I also dreaded the probability that I was going to fail and be either dumped as a patrol officer or knocked down to the lowest possible rank.

Nor was this an ordinary campus, full of excitable young radicals and beatniks. For example, Tom Ellis, who we elected as our student representative, had been a wartime pilot. Before that he had been stationed for some years in New Guinea, and was what was known up there as a 'Before' (a before-the-war veteran). Tom wasn't inclined to put up with what he termed 'know all' academics, and even less with eager but naive 21-year-olds from the Northern Territory. He was certainly impressive, although some of the others gave the impression that he ought to have been a lot higher than a patrol officer given his age and length of time in the service. Perhaps he had a bit of a chip on his shoulder because of this; even so, he certainly wasn't to be trifled with. As it turned out, when our year at ASOPA finished he was rapidly promoted to District Officer and later became a District Commissioner.

Indeed, all the New Guinea men on the course had had at least four years' solid experience spent in some very rugged and tough country. They had all seen real danger and confronted serious tests of their courage. One or two had arrow wounds attesting to encounters with the then primitive New Guineans, Papuans or Islanders.

There was a temptation for young blokes such as myself to transfer to New Guinea, as it had a great deal more romance than the Northern Territory, and frankly, that was what many of us were after. Altruistic social work or missionary notions about saving the natives were thin on the ground among our set; we wanted adventure and a change from the mundane. So there was something of an inferiority complex among the Northern Territory men, and initially we waited for the barbs and jibes. We were, in essence, mere welfare officers, whereas the New Guinea men were genuine patrol officers, going on foot patrol in uncharted territory for weeks, even months, leading troops of police. They carried guns for shooting people, and they used them.

They had pistols and .303s. We had a .22 for shooting mangy dogs. Among this lot I felt quite insignificant. However, it was only a fortnight or so before we all settled into our course and the New Guinea men learned to like us.

With the start of lectures it soon became apparent that the course was to be a heavy one. There were five subjects: anthropology, government, history of the colonies and the territories, legal studies and geography. The lecturers included Professor A. P. Elkin and the equally famous poet and writer James McAuley, later Professor, who lectured us on government. We looked at how British colonies had been run and the principles of democratic government – we were thinking very much along colonialist lines.

Because there were only twenty-six students, we could call on the lecturers whenever we wanted, and at the end of the day, we'd all go down to the pub together. But it wasn't all drinking and larking about. Our studies were conducted as if we were a branch of a university. There was no intention on the part of the school to set up a dummy course for us to waste a year on. We were expected to write lengthy essays and make full use of the specialised library. You can imagine how delighted and horrified I was; after my innumerable failed attempts to matriculate, here I was practically at university. I didn't know whether to laugh or cry.

The money softened the blow. I was already on a very good salary for those days (about £800 a year), getting more pay than most young people of my age, and while at ASOPA I was also given accommodation. Granted, this accommodation was in an old army barracks, but it was free, and we all had our own rooms. All our number were on full pay plus allowances for being in a capital city. I couldn't have managed better if I'd tried. And although we were students, we had no intention whatsoever of living the miserable life that students normally led. The Government's generosity afforded us ample scope to live the delights of Sydney to the full. So there I was, at twenty-one, with my newly purchased pork-pie hat and reefer jacket, both from Henry Bucks, ready to take on the world.

Sydney was soon far more familiar to me than Melbourne had been. I didn't bother going out to Palmer Street again, but the city had many other charms. Everything seemed so loud, fast and frenetic. It was strange to be surrounded by so many white faces, on the street, in church, in the pubs.

We had a number of favoured watering holes in Sydney, such as the Clifton Gardens and the Mosman Junction hotels. In Sydney proper, Ushers Hotel was a favourite of the New Guinea men. Its New Guinea bar kept a steady supply of *the* PNG drink, Rhum Negrita. The bar also kept a register for PNG visitors to record their Sydney addresses. Many festivities began at the New Guinea bar after visitors on leave were discovered through that register. Lots of them ended up at the many parties held at ASOPA.

As a group, the New Guinea blokes were a pretty solid bunch with very independent and adventurous spirits. At times they were a bit difficult to control, but as they all held the rank of sub-inspectors of police, exuberance was kept within reason. On one occasion, however, a drinking session at Ushers provoked that time-worn act of booze-induced larrikinism, and an empty tram parked behind Wynyard Station was boarded and driven about fifty yards up the road.

The only time exuberance got me into any trouble was when I was away from my ASOPA friends and drinking with friends from the Manly Surf Club. They had a reciprocal agreement with my Point Lonsdale Surf Club and I'd been sure to keep up my membership. On Saturday we were up at the North Steyne pub, and got into trouble with a bloke called Bonehead who liked a fight. After a few whacks and a scuffle, I was rescued by some who knew what Bonehead was like, and for my troubles I was taken to a beaut party at the Newport Hotel, which went all night.

I liked a drink as much as most of my mates, but I had good reason now to keep things in moderation. Since my National Service on the aircraft carrier HMAS *Vengeance*, enviously admiring the young fleet air-arm pilots, I had dearly wanted to learn to fly. Here at last, with ample time and money at my disposal, was my opportunity.

I enrolled with the Illawarra Flying School out in the western Sydney suburb of Bankstown and took lessons on the weekends and occasional weekdays. It was fairly expensive (about £8 an hour), and two to three hours a week was all I could afford. Bankstown's flying schools favoured Austers, and the craft I normally used was a red high-wing monoplane powered by a Gypsy Major engine. I wasn't a natural pilot and took a bit longer to go solo than many others, although given my less-than-inspiring academic record, any study achievements warranted registration in the miracles category. Nevertheless, it was almost certain that I would never have won my wings in the fleet air-arm.

Still, it was one of my most thrilling experiences when the instructor hopped out of the aircraft one day, taking with him the detachable dual joy-stick, and told me to get going and do a circuit by myself before he changed his mind. I remember having a strong urge to fly under the Sydney Harbour Bridge, which was clearly visible at the circuit height of one thousand feet. I resisted the urge and landed instead. My very patient instructor pandered to my youthful euphoria by pinning upon my jacket the solo wings . . . then sent me straight up again to do another solo circuit. Again I let the Harbour Bridge alone.

By August I had passed all the required exams and had gained my private pilot's licence. This was in no small part thanks to the fearsome Tom Ellis, who spent a good deal of his own time teaching me the use of the Dalton computer and the theory of the triangle of velocities. Not wishing to leave readers with the impression that I had now uncovered a natural genius for mathematics that had for so long stayed dormant, I should recount the incident, shortly after gaining my licence, when I lost all sense of where I was while flying solo from Kurrajong to Mittagong. Despite my new-found mathematical abilities panic set in. Surveying the ground, I saw what looked like an old war time airstrip and, on circling it, noticed a car parked on the side. Across the airstrip was a wire fence, which I narrowly scraped over. In breach of any number of regulations I landed, much to the surprise of the car's owner, who had been teaching his wife to drive on what he thought was an abandoned air-strip – in the grounds of a girls' boarding school.

Study was hard, and in many ways I was helped along by the discipline that I had to follow in learning how to fly, which flowed on to other subjects. Still, I wasn't overly confident of passing, as many a time I left the lecture rooms completely at a loss. I didn't feel like confiding in the others about my lack of confidence, particularly as it never looked good to be too concerned about your work. That was for swots, not for men. Even so, there was many a night that Ted or Jerry or Tom passed up the beckoning call of the Clifton Gardens for a quiet evening hunched over the books, with only a desk lamp for company.

A month into the academic year, we learned that each six weeks ASOPA ran a short course for female personnel headed for New Guinea, including nurses and typists. The single men quickly arranged to organise parties at the beginning of each of these courses. These turned out to be a quite successful means of keeping us supplied with female company throughout the year. Not wishing to appear churlish, we also organised parties at the end of the course to say goodbye. The get-togethers were particularly welcomed by the New Guinea men, who wouldn't have much of an opportunity to meet available white women once they were back in PNG. This was their big chance. Even the constitutionally nervous types like myself were able to meet women this way, and my flying weekends were an added bonus for women who wanted a date with a difference.

In late November I sat for my exam. The experience I had gained through my flying studies was of immeasurable help in preparing me for the academic crunch, yet I still entered the examination room with far more trepidation than some of my colleagues. I had already submitted my main essays, on the moiety sub-groups in Aboriginal language groups and some other stuff, for 'Government Jim' McAuley about the problems of growing ground nuts in West Africa. Even though none of my papers was immediately relevant to my life, I could see more point in this sort of work than I ever could with anything I'd done at school, and so I felt relatively confident with these essays. Even so, I had a track record of coming unstuck when the clock was ticking against me, and this was not the time to get cocky.

The results came through about the second week in December, and beforehand, the word got out that all but one of us had passed. Waiting on the morning of the results was a personal hell. I was resigned to failure, allowing myself not so much as a glimmer of hope that I'd passed, just so I wouldn't be disappointed or shocked when the news came through. When the results were posted, no one was as surprised as me to see that I'd not only passed, but out of twenty-six students, I'd come sixth.

Paul Hasluck, the Minister for Territories, came to the school in his black car, spouted some politician's twaddle and presented us all with our Certificates of Pacific Administration. It was an amazing moment, and I so much wished that Mum and Dad could have been there. But none of the others had invited their families – it just didn't seem the right thing to do.

Although I only realised it dimly then, ASOPA had set us up with a framework for debate and discussion on what we were actually doing up north, what our roles were as welfare and patrol officers, and how a real politics of Aboriginal affairs could develop. Such questions were rarely considered on the ground, and the vast distances that separated many of us during our working time made it even harder.

The break-up week was a notoriously boozy one, even though most of us would be seeing each other back in our respective territories. We bid farewell to each other, then went our separate ways. I was entitled to four weeks' leave, and I hankered after a sea trip, so I took the three-day voyage on the S.S. *Kanimbla* to Melbourne. My father had served on this ship as a chief petty officer when it was a troop carrier returning Australians from Europe (it later ferried the occupation forces to and from Japan), so it was with some degree of pleasure that he met me at Port Melbourne, a few days before Christmas.

I spent the break travelling between Williamstown and Point Lonsdale, doing my requisite surf patrols (I'd kept up my membership while I was away) and joining in a lot of surf club fun. Having been away, I wasn't a regular competitor, although I had a go in beach sprints and open surf races. Of course they all wanted to know what I'd got up to in Sydney and the Territory which led me to imitate Ted Egan's version of the corroboree dance in the sand dunes at Point Lonsdale on New Year's Eve.

I had a few opportunities to show off my new-found skills. There was a circus at Point Lonsdale that year, with a camel tethered behind the dunes. Macka McKinnon and I decided to steal it, but we couldn't get the camel to move. We pulled on the rope at its mouth, to no satisfaction, so I tickled (or rasped) the camel's genitals with some tea-tree prickles, and it certainly moved then. Macka was very impressed with my bushman's skills! We took it all the way to Ocean Grove, where we left it tethered outside a party.

I knew I had many lonely months ahead of me when I returned north, so I relished every moment at Point Lonsdale. Once again, I boarded the plane for the Territory with mixed feelings.

CHAPTER 8

The one certainty of my job as cadet patrol officer was that there was always something new around the corner. No sooner had I returned to Darwin from Sydney in January 1957 than I was sent on my next posting: the government settlement at Snake Bay on Melville Island.

The Dragon Rapide aircraft with the fortnightly mail and rations left Darwin early in the morning when I travelled to Snake Bay in the last week of January. I was immediately reminded of the realities of life up north as soon as I boarded. In those days, if Aboriginals were flying, planes didn't have seats attached, as the Aboriginals were sat on the floor. Naturally, the same didn't apply to Europeans, who had to be provided with a seat. In New Guinea, planes were actually licensed for a given number of seated Europeans, or a greater number of unseated natives. On this flight, all seats except one – for me – had been removed. The remaining space was filled with rations, mail for Snake Bay and an Aboriginal man who was being repatriated from the Darwin hospital.

Given the importance of air travel in the north for transport and communications, I had emphasised in my post-ASOPA report to the Department that I had now qualified as a pilot, in the hope that this skill could be used in my work. I had forgotten about the red tape and regulations of public service guidelines, and my not-so-gentle hint came to nought. This was depressing: I had had visions of myself as Biggles of the North. It's not too difficult to see how flying would have been a great asset in the Northern Territory, but it was obviously too difficult for the Department to see.

Melville Island is to the north of Darwin and is said to be the biggest island other than Tasmania off the Australian coastline. Together with Bathurst Island, from which it is separated by the Apsley Strait, it is inhabited by the Tiwi peoples. These Aboriginals speak a language completely different from that of the mainlanders, have a very dark 'blue black' complexion and were a very contented community.

About a thousand Tiwis lived at Bathurst Island, centred on a well established Catholic mission run by the Sacred Heart order of priests and nuns. There were two other European-controlled communities on Melville Island: one at Garden Point, which was run as an orphanage for girls under the care of nuns from the mission at Bathurst Island, and the other a government settlement at Snake Bay on the north coast.

The government centre housed about two hundred and fifty Tiwis. In charge of the settlement was a superintendent, Paul Ingram, and his wife Tessa. A schoolhouse was under the charge of Sandy McKay, brother of Jock McKay of Mainoru station.

The buildings were basic, but appropriate for the setting and needs. Just off the picturesque bayside beach was the superintendent's house, and a store with another small residence. Attached to the schoolhouse was a residence for Sandy and an ablution block for the school children. A further house, spare at the time that I was there, had been built for an assistant superintendent or manager. Further along from the settlement was a timber mill and a fruit and vegetable garden. A goat herd wandered about the place, and further inland there were some wild cattle, pigs and buffalo. The seas abounded with fish and the rocks were plentifully supplied with oysters. To be posted to this tropical paradise was fortune indeed.

By some quirk of fate Hilda and Agnes from Beswick settlement were also here. Hilda's husband Nipper had had to leave Beswick and was happy to come over to Snake Bay. He took my gear over to the empty assistant superintendent's house where Agnes had already made up a bed and had the place ready. The verandah looked out over the beach and across the bay. The contrast with the arid life of the outback could not have been more stark.

Back at Paul's house, Tessa had prepared a lunch of cold goat meat, oysters, fresh fruit from the garden and home-made bread. Tessa was an excellent cook, using garlic, ginger, capsicums, olive oil and all the culinary delights that had still not made their appearances in the Australian diet. These were all new to me. Certainly such exotica were never used by my mother. This, combined with an excellent vegetable garden and a never ending supply of fresh fish and oysters, made dining a pleasure at the Ingrams. Tessa taught me quite a lot about cooking.

The first evening was a 'getting to know you' affair with Sandy, who normally kept to himself, coming up for a drink. Sandy was thinly built with a ruddy complexion, grey balding pate and a wrinkled brow. As one would expect, whenever the fortnightly plane came over from Darwin with mail and rations, there was also a delivery of liquor. Sandy came up to collect his rum and we all settled in for a drink on Paul's verandah, enjoying a splendid tropical evening under a canopy of very bright stars, after which I turned in, drifting off to sleep to the sound of waves lapping on the sand and the clack clack clack of corroboree sticks.

The next morning I awoke to the giggles of Agnes, a girl with whom I felt some 'chemistry'. She had brought me a cup of tea, but seeing I was naked with the sheets not properly covering me, she remained at the door giggling 'Tea boss, me bringem tea boss'. What the brothers at Assumption College called 'impure thoughts', went through my mind. I don't know who was the more embarrassed.

Agnes was by now sixteen or seventeen years old, with a big open smile showing white teeth, contrasting with her attractive shiny blue-black face. She'd not yet been 'promised' to anyone in marriage, and not having had a child had kept her figure. I never worked out who her real family was. Hilda was not her true mother and

Nipper came from a different tribe. Hilda and Nipper had become her guardians when Agnes was very young in Darwin. Probably it was due to this unorthodox family set-up that she had not been 'promised'.

At breakfast Paul and I discussed what my tasks were to be during my stay. I could see that I was becoming quite well-rounded in my skills as I moved from assignment to assignment. One of the major projects here was building a jetty on the southern side of the island at Calico Creek. Boats from Darwin could save a day each way by depositing cargo at the new jetty and then the settlement truck could pick it up and drive it across the island to Snake Bay. This also meant that we would have to make the track across the island reasonably bog proof during the wet season, particularly in the low country known as 'Emu Plains' in the middle of the island.

First, however, I was to go immediately to Calico Creek and supervise the construction of the jetty. We hoped that one of the first boats to use it would bring across the four-wheel drive that the island had long waited for. For the jetty's construction, Paul had a team of natives, well trained, but needing supervision lest they wander off. I was to be the supervisor – another new experience.

My diary entry for Friday 1 February 1957 reads:

Helped with rations and repairs to tractor. Left for Calico Creek to work on jetty. Bogged down and camped on Emu Plains.

After breakfast Paul and I set off on a tractor for Calico Creek. Calico Creek was a tidal estuary with a differential between high and low water as much as fifteen feet. Paul's construction technique was to wait until the tide went out and then quickly sink as many piles as possible, so the differential was vital.

> Saturday 2 February: *Cleared tractors out of bog, attempted to clear Chev but failed and abandoned it. Had lunch at Taracumbie (a beautiful spot with a waterfall, on the track between Calico Creek and Snake Bay). Reached Calico Creek early in afternoon and worked on jetty. Made camp about two miles from creek on site of native camp. Roast pigeon for dinner.*

Hilda's husband Nipper adopted me and appointed himself the curator of my well being. Thanks to Nipper my camp site was well organised and clean. First thing each morning my fire was going and billy boiling, without any trouble at all, even if there had been a storm during the night. On my first night there, the men shot a lot of bush pigeons, which we roasted for our dinner – pleasant enough, but too bony; certainly not as good as the bush turkeys we had at Beswick.

The people here seemed much happier than those back on the mainland. They had never lost their land, and they didn't have cattle station owners telling them what they had to do. It was still a complete society. They didn't want for food. There was no liquor at all, no unscrupulous whites selling them grog. Their isolation had served them well.

Ali Sawmill had milled much of the timber for the jetty decking at Snake Bay and had taken it across. Ali was a true character. He loved dressing up in corroboree paint and often had feathers in his hair. He always pushed himself forward when visitors came to the island, spinning a lot of yarns to unwary amateurs or anthropologists.

I was later to witness an amusing instance of this. One anthropologist was quizzing Ali about the large holes that were cut into the ends of Tiwi burial posts, wondering whether the holes were for the spirits of the dead to see out from. Without turning a hair, Ali agreed, adding that only the happy spirits were allowed to use the holes in this way. Afterwards I said to Ali that his story sounded like a lot of nonsense. He had no wish to argue with that. As he well knew, the main reason the very large holes were cut out of the tree trunks was to make them lighter to carry from the bush to the funeral site. Ali simply couldn't resist fooling this earnest anthropologist.

Paul left after a couple of nights, and I was now in charge. Building a jetty is an unlikely basis for adventure, but I had all the necessary provisions. As I wrote to Mum and Dad at the completion of the work, 'The (Welfare) Branch have come good with some excellent camping equipment, so I have come into the possession of a sleeping bag, blankets, axe, tucker box and all manner of things. For several days I was out there by myself with about a dozen natives, living like an Abo myself.'

> Tuesday 5 February: *Began work on piles and sunk ten. Lads worked very well and were quite friendly. Ate pigeons again. Getting no better with the sandflies. Nipper elected himself my batman and brought up tea at dawn and generally kept my tent clean, in addition to working on wharf and preparing my meals.*

> Wednesday 6 February: *Sunk remaining six piles by early afternoon. Let the boys have rest of day off. Issued some ammunition to enable them to hunt. Tasted wallaby meat for lunch.*

Sixteen piles in two days was a pretty fair effort so we all had some time off. I issued the men with ammunition and lent them my rifle, hoping that they would return with something decent to eat. They returned with a wallaby for their evening meal, but no bush turkey. Wallaby cooked in the manner of the Aboriginal does not appeal to me as it is too raw and smoky. And as it has been neither bled nor hung for any time at all it is tough and gamy.

To cook any animal Aboriginals simply place it on the embers of a fire, whole, without any preparation at all. The animal is not skinned nor are its entrails removed.

When much of the fur is burnt off, the carcass is then covered with the embers. There are, of course, no condiments! After a time someone grabs the tail and shakes the embers off. The stomach is then opened and people – in an orderly fashion – take out bits of offal to eat. The legs are often kept for later as they can easily be carried. Pieces of the body are cut off and dipped in the blood of the carcass that is still laying open on the fire. At times portions are put back on the fire for more cooking.

I stuck to the salt beef stew. Salt beef is no delight but it is easily transported and keeps for a very long time even in the heat without refrigeration. Preparing a salt beef meal is quite a ritual as it must be boiled a couple of times to get the salt out and the beef tenderised. If I'd had more experience I would perhaps have selected a cut of the wallaby and stewed or broiled it the next day.

While the men were working I decided to walk to Cockle Point. Ali Sawmill escorted me the four or five miles to where Calico Creek entered Apsley Straits. Ali, like many Aboriginals was a very fast walker and even though I was a lot younger it took a fair bit of effort to keep up with him.

On arrival at the coast Ali took me to a native camp where he ate a bit of the cold wallaby that he'd brought with him. The natives at this camp had a fire going and so the wallaby leg was re-cooked upon the embers around the fire's perimeter. In an attempt to be social I tried some, but only a couple of bites. Instead I ate a small whole fish that had just been caught by one of the men in the camp.

Ali seemed to know everyone at the camp and he was able to organise a dugout canoe (with paddlers) to carry me across to the Catholic mission on the other side of the straits on Bathurst Island. (I wanted to introduce myself to the Fathers and, as a Catholic, was still drawn to the church.) The straits are only about a mile across but as the tide runs very quickly in those parts, the paddlers of the canoe had to head into the tide by quite a few compass points to land us at the mission. Because of this, considerable spray was blown into the canoe. Since being on the island I had been growing a beard and so I must have looked like an escaped prisoner as I strolled up from the beach to the presbytery, wet, bedraggled, unshaven, unannounced and carrying a rifle.

The Bathurst Island Mission had been established for many years and many fine buildings were set among the pleasant gardens and its striking palm trees. The charming timber church had high cathedral ceilings, louvred walls and a sanctuary and altar whose design blended Roman Catholic and Tiwi culture. The presbytery, convent school, and store buildings were all well-maintained and built of local timber, not at all like the plain stereotypical buildings that were found on government settlements.

Although I thought that I was unannounced, I had not taken into consideration the remarkable 'bush telegraph', and news that a 'whitefella' had arrived by canoe had reached the presbytery ahead of me. As I loped up the path, I could already see a priest waiting. This was the engaging and robust superior, Father Cosgrove. He received me enthusiastically, much of his welcome directed at getting this sodden arrival showered and changed.

Living in the presbytery with Father Cosgrove were two lay brothers, Brother McCarthy and Brother Bush. That made three. The fourth member of the community was away, an unacceptable situation for they were, of course, one short for cards. Brother McCarthy felt it important that I should stay the night and so make up a four for cards that evening. There seemed to be some urgency in his invitation. Brother McCarthy was a fearsome gambler . . . of sorts. On Saturdays he'd be glued to the radio trying to pick up distant races and tallying his imaginary bets. The arrival of a possible fourth for cards was therefore not to be left unexploited.

The evening meal in the refectory was served by Aboriginal girls, who to my surprise wore blue skirts, but no tops. Cossy, as Father Cosgrove was known, said that the local nuns saw no reason for the girls to depart from their traditional ways, particularly in a tropical setting, unless they were married. In fact, he said, single girls had been allowed to dress this way at Bathurst Island since the early days when the mission had been founded by Monsignor Gsell.

This was all well and good in theory, and showed a greater understanding of traditional ways than was usually found in missions, but I found it virtually impossible not to look at these young women in a sexual way, despite (or because of) generations of impacted Catholic guilt. And I wondered how the clergy – celibates all – put up with it. It didn't seem to worry them, which struck me as quite odd. I didn't stare, but many was the time I sneaked a second look.

After the evening meal. I went to confession. It was the first time I had been for some time, and the setting encouraged me to think a little about my vocation. I'd long since realised that I wasn't cut out for celibacy, even though that was still the state I was in. But I enjoyed discussing theological matters, and on this night and during the many pleasant dinners and evenings that came later on, I picked up quite a bit of the history and philosophy of the mission. Cossy had a practical and realistic approach to incorporating Christianity with Aboriginal culture, which he had inherited from the enlightened and non-puritanical philosophy of his predecessors at the mission. Unlike many church workers in Aboriginal communities Cossy did not rail against all things Aboriginal, but tried to use as much of their culture as was possible, in line with his own view of Christianity.

For Cossy, the Dreamtime and Biblical creation were not in conflict. He saw no reason why some of the traditional songs and legends of the Aboriginal people could not blend in comfortably with the creation story of the Bible. And of course, Cossy and his predecessors had good reason to pay tribute to Tiwi cultural values. Traditional beliefs were still very strong on the island, as one could easily tell from the large number of funeral poles that were dotted around the settlement.

The burial and mourning customs of the Tiwi were a protracted and much ritualised affair, generally referred to by the word *pukamuni*. After a death, the closest of the deceased's relatives were not allowed to use the dead person's name, could not touch food with their hands and had certain rituals to perform until the following wet season. These were accompanied by wailing and skin cutting by the mourners, the more blood and crying the better the mourner. At the appropriate time the funeral poles were set up and additional ones were added at various anniversaries.

At some masses, Cossy had tried to encourage Aboriginal chanting accompanied by the cadence of the clacking sticks. In his view, that Aboriginal ceremonial was very much a worship or acknowledgement of God in His creation. Obviously, Aboriginal views on procreation and polygamy did not sit too well with either the Catholic faith or our Western knowledge of biology. In part this conflict had already been overcome by Monsignor Gsell, the mission's founder.

This astute priest had come to grips with the tribal custom of old men owning many women of descending ages by acquiring over some time the rights to many of the young girls, as if they had become his own property. Not long after the mission was established in 1911, a young girl named Martina, in fear of her violent husband-to-be, sought the protection of the mission. The answer was not simply to remove the girl from her environment, as Monsignor Gsell well knew the tribal obligations. After much haggling, the old man and tribal elders permitted

Monsignor Gsell to acquire the rights over Martina in exchange for various items from the mission store.

The old men who were too frail to hunt, had in the past, as on mainland Australia, been used to trading some of their younger wives to be 'sweethearted' by younger men in exchange for prestige and food. So, from that time on, whenever the opportunity presented itself, similar 'purchases' were made by the Monsignor. He then encouraged young men to purchase the young women off him and marry them, providing this was in accordance with Aboriginal law, and on the condition that each man married only one girl.

Over time a relatively monogamous community was established among the Tiwi on Bathurst Island. Towards the end of Gsell's life, a book was written concerning this clever adaptation of things tribal and Christian, entitled *The Bishop with 150 Wives*.

How much the natives genuinely embraced Christianity was hard to determine. Cossy's adaptations obviously made Christianity more familiar and acceptable to many Aboriginals, but the weight and influence of an institution often creates conversions of convenience.

The story was told of a mission in Arnhem Land that issued a weekly supply of 'backy' (a cheap plug tobacco used by whites throughout the Territory to pay Aboriginals) on Sundays. Understandably everyone attended church on Sunday. On this one occasion the box of backy was emptied before one old man had received his plug. 'No more'im backy, no more'im Jesus,' he said, and returned to the camp.

I don't know how many, if any, genuine converts to Christianity were made by the various missions, but I felt that most of the missions did more good than harm. They taught reading and writing many decades before we did. When they worked, they were really the forerunners of the government settlements that we were now establishing.

> Thursday 7 February: *Rose too late for Mass. Had breakfast and talk with Father Cosgrove. Father has many good ideas on genealogies and giving natives surnames. His idea is to find the name of some native who has been dead long enough for it to be used and then call all the person's descendants by that name. Canoed and walked back to camp. Had lads cut logs into stumps for future store shed.*

By the following morning, the boys had sunk quite a few pylons into the creek bed, so ammunition and rifles were again issued. By midday plenty of pigeons, a snake, a wallaby and some fish were available as a supplement to salt beef, tinned food, potatoes, rice and onions. I tentatively ate some of the snake but settled for a pigeon stew.

Bernard arrived on a tractor with additional rations. Bernard was one of the settlement's more accomplished citizens, and could read, write and relay messages as well as work on motor vehicles. On one occasion I was without matches and wanted a fire. The Tiwi traditionally made fire by twirling a hardwood stick into a piece of softer wood, so I called in Bernard, expecting him to do his time-worn stuff. Instead, he rustled up some bark, dipped it into a petrol tank, undid a spark plug from a vehicle, left its lead on, and turned the motor over.

However much I enjoyed the company of the Aboriginal men, I found it difficult to have in-depth talks with them. There was an obvious language problem and, of course, our worlds were far apart. The only things we could talk about were the things we had in common – everyday talk about work. They also had a tendency to be overly willing to please, to say yes, which meant they agreed with everything I said. We floated along on pleasantries.

This wasn't always the case, of course, particularly when it came to practical matters. When the occasion warranted it, the Aboriginals I worked with would show me a better way to dig a posthole or chop a tree. I didn't stand on any dignity and they knew that. At other times I would be driven mad by their carefree attitude towards the things that I felt had to be done. It wasn't all that important to them that we got a road across the island. It wasn't all that important that we got a Land Rover. It wasn't all that important that the aeroplane came in. Their lives went on very much the same regardless. More times than I care to remember I would ask where someone or something was, to be greeted by the inscrutable reply: 'Must be somewhere, Boss.'

Saturday 9 February: *Cooked fried rice. Ali returned from Mission, saying that Father Cosgrove had invited me over for Sunday Mass. Left afternoon by Mr Ingram's 'duck punt' (a metal dinghy with no outboard motor) and rowed down Calico Creek with Murray (a native who has let his hair grow long – altogether a suspicious-looking character. Said he wanted to go to Mass, but I didn't see him there.) Some trouble getting across straits. Dinner & cards as before.*

The following weeks were taken up working on the various agricultural projects that the island needed for self-sufficiency. Under Paul's direction, land was being prepared for maize and sorghum while more peanuts were being planted. Banana and pineapple groves had to be attended to, and the goat herd looked after.

Wednesday 20 March: *Still wet but thought it best to get something done. Had tractor take trailer across Emu and used it for carting timber. Stayed on this job till afternoon tea and returned to Snake Bay. Had some trouble with troops, who, when I had left, stopped working and more or less followed me to the camp where I discovered the position. Talked severely but, I thought, logically to them and they admitted their error. Told them if they had complaints they should let me know, not do things behind my back.*

The work was done intermittently over some months and was fitted around our other jobs. It was made more difficult by the wet weather. Nerves began to fray and tempers were sometimes aroused. Keeping control

Nosepeg, Guy and Tuppa Tuppa in the Kintore Ranges, 1957, farewelling Pintubi country. This is the first time that Guy, a Pintubi Aboriginal, had ever worn clothes.

Bernard holding the door open for 'Uncle' Paul Ingram.

Women at Haasts Bluff gained weight rapidly once their diet changed to western food and the incentive to forage was taken away.

An out-station stock camp at Wave Hill, 1957.

Ration day at Haasts Bluff.

Often there was nothing for the men to do but sit around playing cards or chatting.

Boys at Haasts Bluff wearing government-issue clothes.

Des Morrison and a drover on the Muranji Track, 1957.

*Colin on Murray's boat in the Apsley Straits, Easter 1957.
Waiting for steak and onions.*

*Tuppa Tuppa (left), Nosepeg (middle) and Guy enjoyed a shower
while John Williams (top left) and I luxuriated in Mt Liebig
bore. This was the first time Guy had ever seen this much water.*

Pintubi people stored their belongings high in the trees, away from the dingoes.

We were near Papunya when we killed this snake for tucker.

Kids playing on the donkeys at Haasts Bluff.

Haasts Bluff, 1957.

Ted Evans, Colin, Ted Egan, Lionel Newby and members of the St Mary's football team, Sydney 1956, on board the S.S. Kanimbla.

wasn't usually a problem; until we were joined by someone who had recently arrived home from a spell in Darwin. He saw himself as pretty smart, all decked out with sun glasses and an airforce hat. The day after he arrived we had a particularly difficult morning. After smoko I noticed the new arrival in a huddle with the men. He then approached me and said that the workers in Darwin were on strike, and that therefore the workers here were going to strike. I was amazed at the pointlessness of it all.

It was a difficult moment, but I was sure the men I had working with me did not really understand the meaning of a strike. While I was talking to this smart alec, I indicated to a couple of workers that they should load some boxes near my tent on to the trailer. I kept smiling pleasantly as I addressed the men. When I saw that all the boxes were loaded on the trailer and I was sitting on the tractor I started moving off, saying that they could do what they liked but I had all the tea, sugar, tobacco and other goods. The men all yelled out to stop, which I did. The strike was over. I then sent the troublemaker back to the settlement and we got on with our work.

We finally got the jetty in place and made Emu Plains passable. We all felt relieved to finish and return to the settlement. In such a simple setting, the simple pleasures were the best, and I celebrated my return to 'civilisation' by luxuriating under a shower then indulging myself with clean whites, a cold beer and dinner by Tessa instead of billy stew.

> Saturday 6 April: *Awoken by Mr Ingram with news that Hickey had left. Hasty breakfast and Mr Ingram and self left per tractor 7.45 a.m. Very quick trip, arrived at 10.30 a.m with very sore backside. Unloaded Land Rover and 25 drums of fuel. Christened the new jetty with afternoon 'celebration'. Drove Land Rover home that evening in triumph.*

We had been waiting some weeks for Jack Hickey, certainly one of the Territory's characters, to arrive with the Land Rover on his boat. The men that sailed their own boats around the northern coast line were a breed unto themselves. To a man they relished their independence, enjoyed the many challenges of the sea and their boats. Above all they did things in their own time and would not hesitate to tell anybody to 'go and stick it', if there was any suggestion of being pushed around. By one means or another each of these men had acquired a good seaworthy craft, chartered it when it suited them and gone fishing when they jolly well liked. Yet a fair degree of Territorial commerce up 'the top end' relied upon these latter day buccaneers. Hickey epitomised all of that. Bare-footed, shorts, not even a singlet, tanned, weather beaten and fiercely independent.

On various occasions working out of Darwin I had to sail with Hickey and his rival Jack Murray or meet them down at the wharves to pick up or deliver Aboriginals and cargo. I loved the romance of their environment and found myself laughing a lot when with them. These characters had it all their way as there was much charter work and they were few.

Paul envied Hickey and his way of life but was much exasperated by him. Almost all of our heavy supplies and fuel came by boat and deliveries were at the whim of these casual entrepreneurs. We were told our Land Rover had been sitting on the deck of his boat for about ten days before he decided to make the one-day trip across to Calico Creek. First, it was supposed to be a problem with a key in the propeller shaft, then the fresh water pump. The wet season's unpredictable stormy weather was now hardly an excuse. The four-wheel drive was vital for our small and boggy community.

Paul heard by radio that the Land Rover was at last on its way, so we went down to the new jetty to collect it. Nothing was easy at first. A full tide washing south out of Apsley Straits, accentuated by a stiff breeze, delayed the forty-five foot trawler into the mouth of the creek. Paul and I were rowed out in a flash to help pilot her up the mangrove-lined creek to our precious jetty. This was the culmination of one hell of a lot of work and hopefully the beginning of a new era for the island: a four-wheel drive and a shorter trip for most boat cargo in the future.

Tides dictated that no attempt up Calico Creek would be possible until the beginning of the full tide. Waiting on board was no hardship as Hickey and Paul broached the liquor supplies ordered by us. Henry VIII's progress down the Thames from Hampton Court to Westminster had nothing on this trip up the Calico;

well, that is, except for a nagging anxiety. Were our measurements right? Were the pylons in firmly enough? Assuming these were OK time was then of the essence in order to have the correct juxtaposition of boat and jetty. If the deck of the boat was below that of the jetty it would be impossible to roll the Land Rover off. If we missed a tide then Hickey's craft would end up sitting on the muddy bottom, precariously tied to the untested jetty with our Land Rover lashed to its deck. As it turned out, it went like a dream with Paul sitting in his new toy being pushed ashore to the cheers of the excited workers.

'Corroboree, corroboree' rang out through the Snake Bay settlement, as a holiday was declared to celebrate the arrival of the Land Rover and Paul's good mood. In this instance, corroboree didn't mean anything traditional or tribal but rather a whiteman's festival with the food and soft drink supplied by the store and a lot of 'muck about' dancing.

In such dances Paul and I were expected to try our footwork to the beat of the clacking sticks and the didgeridoo. The didgeridoo was not traditionally used by the Tiwi, but they had adopted it for muck about purposes. Getting painted up was half the fun.

I sat down in the dirt and Ali painted my face and upper body with charcoal and ochre. I was wearing shorts but my feet were bare. Half the joke was that they could use charcoal on me. There was no way it would show up on their dark skin. I'd now seen a few dances, and so could at least keep time with my feet. My efforts were very much solo, with me tagging along behind Ali. Occasionally I'd stand in line and join the muck about. I loved the fun of it all, but I don't think Bernard did, as he saw himself a little more advanced along the white man's path and didn't take part himself. And even though it was a muck about dance, I think he was a touch cross with me for doing it, as it denigrated what he was doing.

The master choreographer was the redoubtable Ali Sawmill. The end of the wet season, the arrival of the Land Rover and Paul in a mood to declare a holiday saw Ali promenading with painted chest and feathers in his hair mustering up support for a dance. He would have made a fortune on the stage.

> Monday 8 April: *Trip to Mission with Mr Ingram. Camped in Calico Creek after having bogged Land Rover.*

> Sunday 21 April: *Went to Mission and took them an 'Easter egg' (rum). Brought back kerosene.*

The end of the wet season also signalled the arrival of The Officials; politicians and senior bureaucrats avoiding the cooler months down south by touring the best spots in the Territory. Snake Bay was on everyone's itinerary. First of the multitude was the Director of Welfare himself, Mr Giese. This protege of the Minister, Paul Hasluck, always felt it necessary to inspect his tropical domain now the 'wet' was over.

Paul Ingram knew in advance that Giese would be inspecting the whole of our operations so Paul, myself and the natives took the opportunity to clean up the camp and the school. My task was the school, so I dropped in on Sandy McKay's classroom a day or so before the Director arrived. On the blackboard was an example of a letter Sandy had written for the children to copy as part of learning English.

> Mr Jock McKay,
> Mainoru Station,
> via Katherine, N.T.
>
> Dear Jock,
> When you come over for Easter be sure and bring plenty of grog.
> Love,
> Sandy

Sandy had lived by himself in the outback for many years. He believed he was doing certain things unbeknown to others, and getting away with them. Perhaps he was. But when he sat at his table pouring cold tea from a teapot, we knew what the brown liquid was.

Then there was Sandy's interest in native hygiene. Like Mrs Allom at Beswick, he was a stickler for showering the children. Unlike Mrs Allom, he paid particular attention to supervising the teenage girls. He claimed this was for the girls' safety, but as time went on, the explanation seemed increasingly dubious.

On one occasion Joe Arthur, a friend of Sandy's who had been a Labor Party Minister in the NSW Parliament, was arguing with him about the onset of puberty, and the age at which it arrived. Sandy called in a young girl and told her to remove her top. 'Look at her,' he said. 'How old do you think this one is?'

Later I talked to Paul and Tessa about the incident. They agreed that he was intrusive, but they insisted that if anything untoward had happened the whole camp would have known and so would they. I doubted their certainty then and doubt it even more now.

Mr Giese came and went. Next on the list was a Swedish journalist and photographer, a Mr Gillsaeter, who stayed on the island for two or three days photographing the funeral posts and the Aboriginal dancing. Ali Sawmill was in his element, and would not let the photographer out of his sight.

Ali organised a terrific corroboree for Mr Gillsaeter (for a handsome fee), and took the opportunity to spin quite a few dubious yarns about the story behind the dance. We were treated to a truly spectacular dance. Ali was painted from head to toe, all ochre and feathers. All the others, women as well as men, were 'dressed' for the occasion. The evening was balmy and tropical, the smoke from the fires drifted in the gentle breeze, and the chanting, the clacking sticks and didgeridoo created a memorable scene.

The Tiwis loved dancing. As in all Aboriginal tribes, the dance was a vital part of the many rituals they had to perform to remain in contact with the Dreamtime, their land and the source of their existence. There were three types of corroboree, roughly speaking. At certain times of the year, or because of a certain event (for example a death), highly organised and secret ceremonials had to be carried out. These were really 'big business', performed by the membership of a particular totem. They were acted out according to a very strict code utilising sacred chants and objects normally hidden, which were brought out for the occasion. Such corroborees were rarely, if ever, seen by non-Aboriginals.

Then there were rituals that could be seen by anyone but were nevertheless performed strictly in accordance with custom. Finally there were the 'muck about' or 'bullshit dances' performed simply for fun. Whitefellas were often invited to these.

The mangrove creeks feeding into Snake Bay were ideal for crocodile shooting. After Mr Gillsaeter had left, Sandy's friend Joe Arthur arrived. This prompted Paul to arrange a crocodile hunt. A couple of dugout canoes, a spotlight, a car battery and some refreshments were organised. Paul was in one canoe with Joe, me, a native, and Paul's .303 rifle, Natives with spears were in the other.

We set off after dark across the bay to the creeks on the other side, and saw quite a few sea snakes and even a shark on the way over. Shortly after reaching the first creek we began playing the light beam along the banks and picked up the eyes of a small croc running into the water towards us attracted by the light. He was dazzled and held in the beam. We could clearly see his two red eyes and the end two rows of knuckles on his back. The middle of the square made by the eyes and the knuckles was the target.

We paddled silently, keeping the croc dazzled until we could shoot almost point blank. Joe held the light and Paul fired. The creek turned the colour of rum. We had shot the croc's top jaw almost off. One of the natives in the other canoe jumped over and with his spear brought the croc's carcass in. It was of no great size, but it had a value, and this would go to the natives. That night we shot three crocs, and possibly killed a fourth, although it wasn't safe to retrieve this last one.

The next morning we skinned the three crocs. The procedure was to cut one incision on either side of the rows of knuckles down their backs and then peel away the skin from both incisions. In this way the valuable underbelly skin wasn't damaged. After skinning, the hides were salted, measured and rolled up, amid non-stop chatter as to the measurements and likely value. A croc skin is measured across the widest part of its girth. In those times skins were worth in the order of 6/- per inch and the men expected about £20 for their evening's fun.

The flesh of the crocs was then taken down to the camp and eaten. Those who eat large amounts of crocodile often emit a certain odour, particularly if they are confined inside a hot building . . . such as a classroom full of children, or a store room. Bad luck for Sandy McKay.

In preparation for important ceremonials food was often stockpiled. One way food was kept available but fresh was by catching large sea turtles and turning them on their backs so they couldn't escape. The killing of a turtle was a well-attended affair. The slaughterman would tap the neck of the turtle with his axe. This would cause the creature's head to spring up in a reflex action. The back of the head would then be given a few swift blows. The under-shell would be opened, leaving the back shell as a container for the turtle's blood. Portions of greeny coloured flesh would be roasted or basted in the blood, which was said to be a great delicacy. I always shuddered when I saw this.

Dugong was another great treat. Expeditions in canoes to catch them were carried out with much preparation, which was almost a ritual in itself. The correct spear with rope attached and a canoe paddled by the fittest men of the community were required Sometimes the dugong hunt would go on for more than a day. A dugong catch was almost enough reason for a corroboree in itself. If, however, the dugong caught was female, the women of the tribe were restricted from eating certain parts of it.

After days of ceremonial no work could be expected. This quiet time was used by Paul to get some office work done or to open up the canteen. The canteen was also opened on pay days. Each fortnight, wages sheets were prepared, listing various names and wages owing. After that figure was a column where the recipient could certify by thumb print that the money had been received. The sheets were sent back to Darwin on the mail plane, to be returned a fortnight later with the appropriate money.

Pay days were a lot of fun, but Paul's method of payment was unorthodox to say the least. He and I would sit at a table next to the canteen. Stretching out in front would be the line of expectant workers eagerly chattering away, mothers with babies, kids running about, and the young men, the nucleus of the workforce, all puffing away on old crab claw shells stuffed with tobacco. Each person would give their 'whitefella' name, receive their money, then impress their thumb print in the column provided on the wages sheet.

In the case of a prized worker such as Bernard, the wages could be as high as 22 shillings, in the case of a lowly paid worker perhaps as little as five shillings. This was fine as it went, but Paul would often decide to change the arrangements midway through. He'd tell someone to 'bugger off', even though their name was on the sheet, if he felt that person had not worked well enough. Paul would then put his own thumb print on the wages sheet. The next in line might be down for 7/6, but if Paul considered he or she had worked hard, then they might get the other person's five shillings as well. The pay sheets, meanwhile, had Paul's thumb prints, and perhaps even one or two of mine, one after the other.

Inevitably Paul ended up allocating more money than he had, which should have meant that some of those in line missed out. Instead, Paul would yell out to me to open up the canteen, and those that had been paid would be encouraged to spend their money. After a few had done so, I'd be told to close the canteen and bring out the takings. These would be used to pay the remaining unpaid workers. The economics of this were mindbending, but it appeared to work. If he found himself short when accounting for canteen sales, he would simply move some items from government stores – items that should have been free of charge – into the canteen and sell them. I would like to think that Paul never personally profited from juggling the books this way, but it was still no way to run a settlement.

Paul was a pragmatic bushman with a good sense of humour and no respect for authority. Sadly, at a later posting at Delissaville he found himself in trouble after gambling in Darwin and was eventually charged and pleaded guilty to some crime of dishonesty. Half of Darwin turned up to give character evidence on his behalf, but Mr Justice Kriewalt sentenced him to some months in Fannie Bay Gaol. I have it on good authority that the indomitable spirit and charm of Paul Ingram was such that the warders assigned him to work as clerk in charge of issuing native stores to Aboriginal prisoners. One suspects he did not enjoy the same opportunity to try out his creative accounting methods.

Easter was approaching. Father Cosgrove had sent a message that I was more than welcome to stay on the mission for the Easter ceremonies. I hitched a ride on the Thursday mail plane from Melville Island to Bathurst Island. The pleasure in Cossy's eyes was transparent when I produced my 'Easter dues' for the church. Four bottles of rum, no less. 'Well,' said

Reverend Father Superior, 'to show there is no ill feeling between church and state I will have a drop'. Lent finished dead on noon Easter Saturday that year.

Tuesday saw the arrival at the mission of Jack Murray, Hickey's shipping rival, with a large number of forty-four gallon drums of fuel destined for Snake Bay. Paul suggested that for this particular cargo it would be better to have Jack sail all the way to Snake Bay rather than unload on our new jetty, and then cart such a heavy load across the still-boggy island. I decided I would sail with Murray from the mission to our settlement.

Time was never Jack Murray's problem so leisurely we made our farewells and pulled away from the mission to get the benefit of the north flooding tide. Jack loved steak and onions so in the twilight after a magnificent sunset, we set anchor in a quiet cove to enjoy his favourite meal. Here I experienced the sheer joy of a still, tropical evening at sea, that the Hickeys and the Murrays shared with very few others. We made Snake Bay mid morning, rolled the drums into the sea and towed them ashore with our local dugout canoes.

Jack Murray then had a problem. Would he go croc shooting or settle for a bit of lazy fishing. The latter suited his mood and so Tessa, Paul and I had yet another blissful evening.

The Aboriginals had a genuine liking for Paul, and called him 'Uncle'. At the same time he could keep control, and knew where to draw a line, keeping himself a respectful distance from them. It was always an interesting sight watching Paul coming ashore or boarding a boat. He would yell out 'Quickly, quickly, who's going to carry Uncle?' to save him getting his boots and socks wet. Nipper or Ali would be first on the scene, to piggyback him through the shallow water. I was never accorded such prestige, and for that I was glad. I was not comfortable with the idea of being carried around.

> Friday 3 May: *Spent day with road gang and put three others to work on fence. Due to their own bad management natives ran out of beef and tea. Very nearly weakened, but finally decided they would eat the whole store if they had the chance so made them suffer for their folly.*

I had a great life with the Tiwi. They still had a living language and culture. They had their land to themselves, with only a few whitemen to bother about. They caught fish, hunted, danced the sacred and the muck around dances. They listened to the songs of the songmen and buried and mourned their dead in accordance with timeless Pukamuni of the Dreamtime.

In the 1980s and mid-1990s, I returned to see the Tiwi paradise, as it is sometimes called in travel brochures. Bread was flown in from Darwin, along with grog, tinned food, and pension cheques. There was a white person to assist in the councils of the islands, some others to organise the Alcoholics Anonymous program, and white school teachers and medical staff with their supporting clerical personnel. There were no canoes in sight, no new grave poles, the gardens did not seem attended, and the sawmill was in ruins.

CHAPTER 9

On my return to Darwin, I stayed at the town mess, a wartime relic that had once been an extension off the navy wardroom. The rooms we were staying in were described as being nestled in a garden setting; what this meant was that the garden came inside our rooms. The showers and toilets were almost permanently occupied by large green frogs which weren't willing to share the accommodation. Bloody-minded cruelty and dexterity with the toilet brush was needed any time we ventured into their territory.

Another pest was lodged in the room next to mine: George, a former British civil servant who had done time in India and Ceylon and was determined to let everyone know this. He was now a clerk in the Health Department, but he never let his lowly status stand in the way of a good bragging session. His hackneyed colonialist attitude and toffee-nosed accent drove everyone mad. When sober he was less than bearable, when drunk, as he was most of the time, he was insufferable.

George was about five foot nine inches in height, with a slender build, thinning grey hair and a ruddy face.

In short, he was a caricature of the pukka bore. To top this off, he was the sort who knew almost everything – or so he said. Whatever you'd done, he'd done better. Whatever you'd seen, he'd seen worse. If you let him talk long enough you might have believed that he should have been the Administrator of the whole bloody Territory – after all, according to him he'd run India singlehandedly.

The worst part of this was that George and I shared a common shower. Nothing was more calculated to drive me insane than hearing him chattering to himself under the shower and then going mad at a bloody big green frog that would be hopping around his toes. The snow-white towel-draped carcass that subsequently emanated from the shower, dripping and ghost-like, was always guaranteed to drive me out of my room, whatever I was doing at the time.

It wouldn't have been so bad had the shower been off his room. The trouble was, to get to the shower he had to come through my room, which meant that George's bad shower experiences were always a prelude for a torrent of whingeing. In fact, he had no separate entrance to his room, so my room was always the way into his.

George on his own was bad enough, but he often brought through a couple of drunken pommy mates who always took the opportunity when passing through to let me know how we should be handling the 'bloody blacks'. Fortunately, George's low-ranking public service position gave him no power whatsoever over those whom he unhesitatingly dismissed as his inferiors. I would have told him to take a look in the mirror, but the mirror was in my room.

Not much had happened in my absence. I'd grown a beard, which made the local paper, so something must have been known about me, and news must have been thin on the ground. There were no new patrol officers; I was still the most junior. I was just about to be promoted to a full patrol officer, no longer a cadet.

Ted Evans was still distant, even though I'd learnt to see his good side. He was dedicated to the Aboriginal cause. He loved his work and the Aboriginals loved him. Yet he did his best to keep his good side covered, usually through binge-drinking. He had to be helped back to the mess sometimes, after he'd had too much to drink, which was a pity. He didn't turn violent, but it took some of his edge off to see him tired and drunk. He really wanted a wife, but he felt as though he'd missed that boat.

A stir was up at the office. A native, Giaka, had been seriously speared out at Groote Eylandt. His brother, Jaboma, believed that he'd been 'promised' a certain young girl, but suspected that Giaka had 'sweethearted longa that fella girl', so a ritual spearing had to take place. This was meant to follow a set order. The parties, including the offender, painted themselves with corroboree ochres and then the offender would duck around and avoid a spear or two. Eventually, he would have to meet his fate – a spear in the thigh if the offence wasn't all that bad or death if it was a serious infringement. By the 1950s, however, a lot of the young bucks weren't going to hang around and be killed just because of a dalliance with some woman who was out of bounds.

Ritual spearings were undoubtedly a valid expression of Aboriginal law. The trouble was they clashed with European law, and so here we were in Darwin to punish a man who had only done what he was expected to do by the standards of his own community.

Giaka was now prepared to make a statement, so I was sent off to the hospital in Darwin to take it. The Magistrate adjourned the proceedings to Giaka's hospital bedside, as it was thought Giaka might die. Poor Giaka! Not only had he been speared, flown in an aeroplane away from his country and friends, tended to by European nurses in a strange environment, but he had also been set upon by Mr Dodds, shorthand writers, lawyers, policemen and me.

In the tin shed that served as a Court House, Jaboma was committed to stand trial. The Supreme Court, surprisingly, later sentenced him to four months in Fannie Bay. Many of us thought a non-custodial sentence would have been more appropriate given the circumstances.

Life in Fannie Bay was very hard on an Aboriginal such as Jaboma used to absolute freedom of movement and the language and company of his tribe. For some town Aboriginals jail in the short-term could be a bit of a joke. Security was very loose for those who knew the system or in particular if one was in a footy team. The footy players were seen at training but always wanted to get back for the evening meal. Fannie Bay was not built to house long-term high-risk prisoners. Sentences of one year or more were served in Yatala prison Adelaide.

> Friday 17 May 1957: *Routine office duties. Left for Batchelor at 2 p.m. to investigate drinking, supplying and cohabiting. Prepared to accost whitemen in act of procuring women. Surprised two men in a car, took their names and had police notified. Caught lubra Alice in room of whiteman Bluey. Took him to the police station and charged him. No sleep, worked right through night. Arrived Darwin 1400 Saturday.*

The Police Department and the Welfare Branch often had to work together if they were to effectively monitor the Welfare Ordinance, but due to that very regulation, they also were frequently opposed to each other. Patrol officers had the right of audience before the courts to act on behalf of wards. On the other hand, as Counsel for the Defence we often found ourselves in conflict with the police.

This resulted in many frustrating clashes, particularly when, in doing the best for our 'clients', we relied upon some technical defect in the police case, such as the accused not being properly gazetted as a ward. As far as the police were concerned, if our 'client' wasn't properly gazetted that was our fault as welfare officers for not properly maintaining the register. It seemed to them that we were having our cake and eating it too, and although we weren't doing this deliberately, one could see their point. We had put them in a no-win situation.

Fortunately, many of the police, such as my friend who'd taken me into the Don Hotel not long after I'd arrived, knew that the problem largely rested with the legislation. Care had to be taken to keep such conflict on a professional level for we had to rely upon the police in many difficult circumstances.

There was the time I was in Rum Jungle, a uranium mine some 100 kilometres south of Darwin. Casual labourers at the mine had been consorting with native women in exchange for liquor, and this was on the endless list of matters to be investigated by the Welfare Branch. Les Penhall, as District Welfare Officer, sent the intrepid Macleod down there to put things right. Pay days at the mine were each fortnight on Thursday, and this was when the transfer of flesh for grog took place, so my visit was timed for best effect.

According to information received by the branch, a certain native, Jimmy Walrus, was known to be one of the area's main providers of women for the purposes of prostitution. Jimmy had three young women as his wives. His practice was to have his ladies ready for marketing to the miners each pay night in exchange for liquor.

With the confidence bestowed by ignorance, I strode into the drunken squalor that was the miners' camp on pay night. I rounded Jimmy and his three women up and let them know in no uncertain terms that I was there to put a halt to their vice and that they were going to help me do it by following my directions. That was part one. Then, after dark had fallen, I positioned them and myself behind a very large banyan tree, near where the exchange of liquor for women was said to take place. Then I waited for action. I soon got it. Along came a black Hillman Minx. Two drunken white miners jumped out and began yelling for Jimmy. In the style of a true agent provocateur, I pushed an unwilling Jimmy out from behind the tree.

'Where's Topsy and Bessie?' one of the miners shouted. 'We've plenty of grog'.

Jimmy was petrified; so petrified in fact that he forgot or ignored the lines I had fed him to fit these two rogues up.

'Me no sell 'em women to whitefellas,' he stuttered.

'But you did last week!'

'Me no more wantem grog,' said Jimmy, nervously backing away.

'Bullshit,' shouted the miner, 'give us Topsy and Bessie. Here's your grog.'

With that, I stepped out from behind the tree in the best of police traditions, shining a torch into the miner's face.

'You are under arrest,' I barked.

'Who the fuckin' hell are you?' he barked back.

It wasn't an unreasonable question. I wasn't in uniform, and I was clearly too small to be a policeman.

'I am Patrol Officer Colin Macleod, and I am arresting you.'

The miner must have thought about this for at least a second or two before he belted me in the face, knocked me to the ground and ran back to the Hillman. His mate was already driving off when he leapt in.

From my new horizontal vantage point I grabbed my torch and noted the Hillman's number plate. By the time I was back on my feet, looking for a pencil and notepad, Jimmy and his girls had disappeared into the bush.

The next day, with the assistance of two large Territory policemen, I went down to the miners' camp, where I found the Hillman Minx and my assailant and his mate. I was now very brave, thanks to my company. I gave the two miners just two options: come with us, which meant a good chance of a hefty fine and perhaps a month in Fannie Bay; or roll your swags and leave the Territory. They were gone within the half-hour. Which was also lucky for me. It was likely that a judge wouldn't have looked too kindly on my one-man vice squad.

Odd as it might seem, it was around this time that I lost my virginity. Nancy was older than me, and was either married or someone's consort – it was never really clear. Because she was with someone else, she knew all the secluded spots to disappear to, and would often commandeer the Land Rover for assignations.

Commandeering was probably in her blood. Blonde, five foot nine, and heavily built, her nickname was Big Nancy. She was one of the clerical girls in the office, and one night she contrived to have me drive her home. On the drive, she made her lunge. Her partner, a plumber, became suspicious and used to try to follow us, but she knew all the tricks to throw him off the scent. The relationship was purely physical for both of us, and after a while it faded without regrets on either side.

Wednesday 22 May: Left Darwin for Warrabri at 0800. Truck in bad condition, returned to garage and had carburettor fixed. Left again 1430, arrived Katherine 2000. Camped on banks of Katherine River. Harold helped with driving.

It wasn't all excitement and punch-ups in the night. The next week's assignment was to take a new truck to a settlement known as Warrabri, which was a few miles south of Tennant Creek. Harold was an experienced driver, so he was deputised to go with me as relief driver and to bail me out of trouble if anything went wrong. All went well down the track and we arrived at Katherine late at night. Harold knew a good spot by the Katherine River where we camped. It was bliss swimming in the cool river water the next morning; just the thing to start the day off well.

As I clambered up the grassy bank my appetite took over. Rather than light a camp fire I thought we could go in to the township and have a full breakfast of bacon and eggs in the cafe that I knew of from my Beswick days. Harold didn't seem too impressed with the prospect, which I took as odd, but I talked him into it and off we went.

When we got to the cafe I ordered bacon, eggs and sausages for two. The hard-faced woman behind the counter fixed me with a disapproving eye.

'Is one of these for your boy?' she asked. She meant Harold.

'Of course it is,' I said. Was she going to throw us out for breaching her unofficial colour bar?

She didn't throw us out. She didn't need to. Instead, she produced two servings of bacon, eggs and sausages: one on china, the other on a tin plate. She took the tin plate outside and indicated to Harold that he could sit under a tree and eat it. Accompanying the tin plate was a pannikin of tea. I was given a cup and saucer.

Neither of us kicked up a fuss; my only feeble act of defiance was to sit outside with my mate, and enjoy our meal together. Such were the customs of the times that neither Harold nor I said anything about it. Many white Territorians in those days wouldn't have even countenanced Harold being served a whiteman's meal. They would rather insist he be 'fed' a chunk of bread and perhaps a tin of bully beef rations kept for the purpose in the tuckerbox.

Harold and I made the ten-mile bore out of Tennant Creek for our evening meal. Roast potatoes and grilled beef over a fire went down very nicely. That night I learned how cold nights could be in the centre as winter approached. Crawling into my swag wearing a shirt and socks was not an experience I had imagined as part of life in the Territory. Harold slept close to the smouldering fire, but that was too smoky for me. I went off to sleep with a chill breeze brushing upon my face, as I peeped out at the brightest stars one could ever imagine.

Warrabri Settlement was still in the throes of construction. At first glance it resembled any other large building site. The name Warrabri was coined from the names of the two main language groups in the area, the Warramunga and the Wailbri. The settlement was intended as a halfway house to assist nomadic tribal Aboriginals merge into the twentieth century. Warrabri was the proud boast and embodiment of the policy of assimilation. It was to be the showpiece of the Welfare Branch, out of which would graduate true assimilants into the Western culture.

By the very nature of assimilation, we thought it would one day end, with everybody happily absorbed into the system, and no Aboriginal culture left in the strictest sense. Professor Elkin thought that ultimately – if assimilation worked out nicely – Aboriginal culture would be preserved in the same way Scots observed Hogmanay or celebrated Burns Night. The Aboriginals would keep their didgeridoos and their dances, but that would be it. They would be Australians and live culturally the same life as Europeans. No more walkabout. People would live in houses. There was plenty of money being put in schools and settlements, we said, so why wouldn't it be so?

That was the theory. Places like Warrabri made a nonsense of it. The site was a miserable affair. Lean-to's of bush timber and scavenged building materials, no toilet facilities, and dozens and dozens of diseased skinny dogs, made for a very depressing introduction to the desert people. The children had runny noses and clusters of flies about their eyes. The adults were sitting around in the dust playing marbles. With little exercise and more food, they soon became fat. A few young men had labouring jobs on the construction site, but in reality employment opportunities were all but nil. Idleness for any community is miserable and dehumanising. How much more so it was for nomadic peoples no longer able to work out their energies foraging for food; now forced to live cheek by jowl with members of another tribe, overseen by functionaries of an alien culture dispensing its largesse as if upon children.

Boredom, coupled with the elimination of one of the essentials of the old way of life, hunting, was rapidly sapping any purpose to life. The daily handouts of food from the store were undermining the younger men's respect for the old men, who were meant to be the repository of ancient ritual, the essential link in the preservation of the food chain. Queuing at the store for a tin of fruit, a bag of flour, sugar, tea, and a handout of meat was far easier than spending hours stalking a wallaby.

Worse, the intrusion of the whiteman's food supply detracted from the old 'songman' in his endeavour to keep alive the richness of the dance, song and ritual of the Dreamtime. Traditional Aboriginals relied absolutely upon religion to carry on the species of animals and plant life. Husbandry of any sort was not within their ken. Professor Elkin had often made the point that the harder it was to eke out a living, the more bloody and desperately determined were the ceremonies. In the centre, where life was so much harder than, say, Melville Island, the ceremonial was carried on with determination, considerable hardship and blood letting.

The classic example of this was the practice of subincision, commonly known as 'whistle cocking'. This painful mark of tribal acceptance required all men at the age of initiation, to have their penises cut along the underside, which inhibited the flow of urine and semen. This custom was very much in vogue at places such as Warrabri.

The couple of days I spent at Warrabri provided me with a lot to think about concerning government policy. I saw lots of problems, but no answers. Whatever happened, tribal people attracted by the apparent ease of European living would continue to arrive. But this undermined and destroyed the religious, political and social life that had existed for thousands of years.

Neither Harold nor I were enamoured with Warrabri so we were not sorry to go. For Harold, the return was more exciting than our trip down as the administration had decreed we could catch the plane up from Tennant Creek. We rolled our swags and were driven into town and met by Creed Lovegrove, the resident patrol officer. I had dinner at his place and Harold was quite at home with some 'boys' camping near by. Our plane was not due in until 3 or 4 am, a pretty rotten hour for Creed to drive us out to the strip. We suggested that he take us out about 10 pm, which he did, then we rolled out swags by the edge of the strip, went to sleep and were awoken by the noise of the plane's arrival in the early hours. Harold was most impressed by the size of the plane and more particularly by the equal treatment he received. Sitting in a seat, with orange juice, coffee and breakfast looking out the window as dawn was breaking were something that my tracker could never have contemplated.

CHAPTER 10

The cattle stations and stock routes to the west of Katherine – Victoria River Downs, Wave Hill and the famous Murranji track – hadn't had a visit from the Welfare Branch since 1954, before the Welfare Ordinance had been put in place. There had long been a staff shortage in the Welfare Branch, and part of the reason for the recruitment drive that brought me in was to ensure that such tasks were carried out.

Ted Evans, the Chief Welfare Officer, was concerned that the cattle barons wouldn't be encouraged to improve the lot of their Aboriginal workers, so a patrol was organised in early 1957. I was thrilled at being out in the bush again, in country steeped in folklore and legend. Here were the biggest properties in the world, properties all but the size of European countries. Forget Luxembourg; some of these properties were more than half the size of Belgium. My enthusiasm increased when I was equipped with a new wooden tuckerbox and a new long wheel base Land Rover. I already had a very good swag and a .22 rifle. The Bagot stores provided plenty of tinned food and cooking utensils, plus a couple of wooden boxes of 'backy', which always came in handy.

Stationed in the township of Elliot was Des Morrison, a patrol officer and one-time Canadian paratrooper, mounted policeman and Ceylonese tea planter. He'd been everywhere and done everything. Inspecting those outback stations and stock routes would be no piece of cake, especially given that the patrol could last six or seven weeks. Ted Evans felt that Des would be ideal, and that I would learn a lot by being his assistant.

Des was a fitness fanatic, and a man of determined character. He always slept on top of his swag, instead of within, wrapping the blankets over and across himself, so if anything happened during the night he could leap up. Most of us would have forever been pulling the blankets back on when we tossed about in our sleep, but Des insisted he had trained himself not to turn over.

He was a funny bloke. One morning I woke to discover I was all alone. No Land Rover, no tracker, no fire, no Des. I was out of my swag in a flash. The sun wasn't yet up, nor even any flies about, and here I was in the middle of the great outback with no food, water or transport. I didn't even have a billy or matches. Then, from behind a clump of mulga, came fits of giggles, followed by the sight of Des and Bullfrog, our tracker, doubled over with laughter.

During the first few days out of Elliot, dust rising through the shimmering heat and scrub heralded the droving plants we soon met. We encountered at least half a dozen 'big mobs' of cattle stretched out along the red dusty track. The Muranji wove its way through hundreds of miles of dry creeks, mulga bush, Mitchell grass plain and spinifex. Rocky outcrops, gullies and mulga stumps always ready to stake a tyre, made the going tough for all upon the track, especially our Land Rover. The occasional stockwhip cracks of Aboriginal stockmen encouraged lagging cows and calves, and kept the strung out mob from detouring too far into the mulga.

Our daily routine didn't allow much respite from hot, dusty and ungraded outback tracks. The cool of the evening often turned into a chilly night, making a camp fire quite a pleasant end to the day's work. Des was a master at preparing a meal using the charcoals on the outskirts of a fire. He did not believe in camping with the drovers, nor did he drink alcohol while on the job.

Enjoyable as camping out was, nevertheless, driving into Top Springs, where there was a store and a cold beer was a relief. We camped at Garibaldi waterhole, not far from the store. Des was happy to be by himself around our camp but I spent an hour or two up at the store yarning with a couple of 'bushies' and the store keeper, savouring every frosty mouthful. It was always a strain conversing with these blokes. They weren't antagonistic towards us, but they didn't have much to say. Most of the drovers were semi-literate at best, and with no radios or newspapers, even trying to talk sport was a virtual impossibility. Conversation was largely limited to recounting the good and bad (usually bad) times that drovers had endured – cattle dying, bores running dry, fences coming down. Many were part-coloured, yet they still spoke of Aboriginals as if they were only half-human. They were puzzled by us because they knew we weren't coppers, but they knew we could also deprive them of their labour force.

Ron Ryan, the Katherine District Welfare Officer, had given me a lot of his old reports of the areas that Des Morrison and I were to traverse, together with a few tips on how to get on with the many strong and independent personalities we would meet along the way. I was warned about Tom Fisher, manager of Wave Hill station. He was well known as a resolutely independent man, not taken with government 'interference'.

There were also highly volatile, almost lawless, drovers, moving mobs of cattle along the hot, dry and dusty tracks; and managers who ran their small properties like medieval fiefdoms. For years these men had laboured with little regard for comforts and niceties and were not over-considerate of their Aboriginal stockmen and their families.

Droving in the 1950s was much as it had been for the preceding fifty or more years. Cattle were driven on the track, watering every second day at one of the waterholes or government bores. Drovers were hardened bush men. Controlling a mob of cattle needed expertise, courage and team work. Controlling the team that controlled the cattle was often harder and crueller. Drovers and station managers were a bit like the old masters of ships under sail, at times brutal, always willing to lead, possessed of native cunning, with hard-won experience and skill at their craft. They worked hard and roughed it with their men.

I felt a thrill seeing the last of these epic Australians move their cattle. But it was also at a real cost to the Aboriginals. A lot of this 'legend' depended on the cheap labour of the 'bloody Abos'. Stories of months on the track without pay abounded. Quite often you'd hear the drovers whine about 'bloody Abos being cheeky and wanting pay'. Just as often workers would be told at the end of the trip, 'Fuck off or I'll blow your head off'.

The Government was determined to ensure at least minimum pay and conditions for Aboriginals in the cattle industry. Over some years the station managers had become dependent on government subsidies to pay native workers. These subsidies and even the licence to employ Aboriginal workers could be withdrawn if an adverse report was filed. The threat of the latter was enough that I don't recall any licence being revoked. We would talk to the stockmen, as union reps talk to members, and even offered sanctuary to badly treated natives and their families on government settlements.

One couldn't expect to change the cattle industry overnight. Some degree of diplomacy and realistic expectations were required. We needed to accept small gains in the hope that the harshest of treatment and the worst of the working and living conditions would be eradicated.

One thing was for sure, the drovers and managers were never in the mood to be pestered by welfare officers. Heaven only knew the whippings, shootings and brutalising that had taken place. Des would speak to the natives while I spoke to the drovers and vice versa. In this way we split our forces and allowed natives to speak in confidence and with candour.

Their tucker was borderline acceptable: damper, beef and tea but almost no tinned and certainly no fresh vegetables. Native stockmen occasionally foraged wild bush tucker, so they showed less vitamin deficiency than their white employers, who displayed the Barkly Rot on their hands and wrists.

We had documentation on the drovers' licences to employ wards and set up their plants. We used this to ensure that when the mob reached its destination, no pay to the men could mean no further licence to the drover. Coupled with this was the increasing recognition among the drovers of the very real power the Welfare Branch exerted among the Aboriginals. We had some control over the future supply of Aboriginal labour. With the need for the licence to employ labour, the days of the press gang were over.

If, for example, West Australian natives were among those from the Territory, or we had queries on subsidy payments for the dependants of stockmen we made radio contact with Darwin. In most instances Des was happy to check out on the food given to the men, and let it be known that the drover would be most foolish if he did not honour his pay obligations.

For the next few days we interviewed drovers. Usually a drover's plant during the day was in two parts. The stockmen and head drover were on horseback moving about the mob, checking upon slow or straying cattle or seeing to a cow that might be in calf or having problems with her offspring. The wagons, sometimes horse drawn, but usually an old wartime 'blitz buggy', with the food, cooking equipment and swags, were either back where the last night's camp had been, or had moved on to an appropriate water supply, to set up the next evening's camp. Mobs on the road could only move about ten miles each day.

Our first major station inspection took us to Wave Hill, then owned by Lord Vestey. It was said to be the second biggest single property in the world. Vesteys owned properties throughout the Territory and Queensland, as well as abattoirs and shipping lines, and enterprises associated with cattle and meat production in other parts of the world. A concern of this size was very influential, and management was not overly fussed by a couple of welfare officers arriving on its doorstep.

When we arrived we were offered accommodation but Des Morrison believed that we ought to maintain our independence until we had completed our inspection and report. I preferred a bed to a swag, but Des was very principled and disciplined and he was my boss. I could see the point he was making. After our inspection was over, we were again offered the hospitality of the homestead, and this time we accepted.

For our inspection, we first checked the maintenance payments, the subsidies received for employing native labour. Then we looked at the payrolls, and spoke to the native workers to ensure all was correct. Then we looked at matters such as clothing, stores, and the general state of the camp. We kept a lookout for children and old people, and if we came across any we telegraphed back to Darwin or sought help for them on the station. If they were sick we might organise an aircraft to take them to Darwin. (Private aircraft did this type of work on government contracts.) Infant welfare hardly existed on most stations, nor formal schooling. Where possible, we encouraged unemployed people or young mothers with children to go to the Hooker Creek settlement, which was progressing well under the direction of Brian Greenfield.

Customarily, cattle stations paid their native station hands and stockmen very little, claiming that they supported the families and relatives of the workers. Such support had more in common with serfdom than welfare.

> Wednesday 10 July: *Inspected camps two and four. Eight natives – all okay. Camps at present situated near water. All well clothed and appear happy. No complaints.*

> Thursday 11 July: *Inspected daily food issues to workers. Mainly bread and beef. Not the best.*

If the Aboriginals at Wave Hill appeared happy, with no complaints, it was largely because they had for so long endured squalid station conditions that they had given up expecting any improvement. The relatives of the workers were kept a respectable distance from the homestead in a filthy camp without running water, proper toilets, cooking or laundry facilities. It was the same old story: skinny sick dogs, flies, miserable humpies, the bored unemployed, the old and frail, the aimless young, all presenting a most wretched pitiful sight. Clothes were the standard khaki trousers and shirts for the men and cotton frocks for the women – mostly ragged and dirty. Workers and former workers had stockmen's elastic sided boots, but bare feet were the norm. They were fairly well-clothed by camp standards.

Tea, flour, sugar, some tinned foods, and a ration of meat from the herd was provided. To see a mess of offal being cooked up in a copper over a fire is not the most appetising sight, much less when it is being ladled out on to dirty tin plates and eaten with fingers by people sitting in the dust, not even bothering to swat the flies, or push away the mangy dogs.

This was a far cry from life as a nomad. Still, the people clung on to some aspects of Aboriginal life. The skin and totem systems were very much alive. Young men were initiated into the tribe by the age old ceremonial, taken away to learn the songs and chants, legends and geography of their 'country'. Taboos were still practised.

Tribal culture was never very far below the surface of station life. A cursory view of Aboriginal life on an outback station could miss this. Decision makers on the stations who disregarded this did a great harm to 'their' Aboriginals and perhaps even to their own organisation.

The contrast between life in the Aboriginal camp and life in the 'big house', the manager's residence, was sharp. After some nights camping out I accepted an invitation to dinner, while Des was away inspecting a small neighbouring station. As I wrote in a letter home:

'Life on the station is rather smooth, beginning with a native bringing one a cup of tea at 6.30 am. The station has two dining rooms, one for the white workmen and one for the manager, overseer and such people as myself. There always seem to be visitors staying here and one is positioned at the table in some sort of order of priority. I have rated about halfway down. The chap sitting next to me is a doctor who is in charge of the Royal Adelaide Hospital, and comes from India.

'When all the ladies are seated the men sit down and the maids bring in the first course. When everyone has finished that, the manager rings a bell, the plates are taken away and the next course brought in. After dinner, everyone adjourns to the "parlour" for tea or coffee and then bed or cards. Canasta seems to be all the rage, so I have become a victim.'

Suspended over this luxurious and well-laden dining table were gently moving punkahs, providing us with a cooling breeze. Unlike the punkahs in the Darwin Club these were not driven by motors, but by young Aboriginal boys pulling ropes. During dinner the scraps were heaped on to tin plates and taken outside for those young boys to eat. As smokers lit up, the draft from the punkahs had to be stopped, so the manager Tom Fisher would stamp on the floor as a signal. The punkah boys began immediately they heard the manager yelling out or again stamp his foot on the floor.

After our inspection, Des had a long hard talk with the manager Tom Fisher. Tom was of the old school, and had seen many hard times of his own, but still he was astute enough to see the way things were going. The issue of Aboriginal welfare was not going to go away, and nor were we, unless he and his kind paid more attention to the needs of his workers. He agreed to employ a couple of men to carry out basic hygiene duties, with particular emphasis on the digging and maintenance of toilet pits. Agreement was also reached on the need to build a better communal kitchen, and include more tinned or dried vegetables in the diet. As the natives in the camp had exhausted any firewood that had been close by, foraging and carrying the wood was becoming more difficult. The management agreed to make available trailers hauled by donkeys. Donkeys ran wild by their hundreds in the outback and were often used for other chores about Wave Hill and several of the cattle stations in the area.

One matter that was always difficult to negotiate was the need for young men to be given time off to carry out their tribal obligations, particularly when it came to initiations. Traditionally, young men were sent off by themselves to learn the art of survival in the bush. At regular intervals older men would meet up with them to see how they were getting on and to give further instructions. Ceremonies, involving circumcision and subincision, could only be performed if the wounds had a chance to heal. The correct procedures could take many months.

These ceremonies clashed with the management's need for young men to be trained in horsemanship and stock control. Wave Hill had many outstations and covered a huge area. It had a continuing need for experienced labour. There was no easy answer to this conflict between the need for station labour and the preservation of Aboriginal culture.

As well, some young men rebelled against their heritage. They no longer saw any point in the ceremonies. The station owners wrongly took this to be a positive development, but we in the Welfare Branch knew how important it was that the fabric of traditional society was maintained. Not only was it vital for the Aboriginals themselves, but without it, discipline within the camp could not be enforced. The older people had a real need to preserve their traditional safeguards and see that the younger men had direction.

Tom Fisher was willing to allow such absences and recognise the core role of ceremonies and traditional lifestyles. The same willingness was not always forthcoming from other stations.

The cattle barons wanted it both ways. On the one hand they rejected interference in their control over Aboriginals, yet they continually labelled them as useless do-nothings who were unworthy of any payment, even after they had worked for weeks on end under very trying conditions.

Until the late 1950s and early 1960s the cattle barons had the best of the situation. The Aboriginals had nowhere to go but their tribal country, upon which the cattle stations were built. They were captives on their own land, in much the same way as English serfs were to the Normans, dependent on the pitiful handouts from their overlords.

The inroads made by native welfare legislation were bitterly resented by the cattle industry. The bigger stations, under managers, tolerated us, knowing they could wield influence in Canberra if they thought that our demands went 'too far'. The smaller stations, closer to the financial knife edge, just wanted us to stay away from 'their Abos'. Such stations made no payments or deducted costs 'incurred' in providing sustenance for their workers' families, leaving a nil balance owing.

The attitude was simple: feed the labour force and its dependants enough to keep them alive, as one did with draught animals, and discourage the sick and old from remaining on the property. Bad luck if those ejected were deprived of family and entry to their sacred sites, which had now been turned over to cattle grazing. Conditions in these stations were appalling.

Throughout July and August 1957, numerous stations were reported upon with varying degrees of praise and criticism. Places such as Newry, Inverway, Rosewood, Limbunya, Auvergne and many others received our attention.

> Friday 2 August: *Auvergne is quite good as regards conditions for the natives' laundry, latrines and accommodation.*

A week later, at another station:

> Sunday 11 August: *Management most unco-operative. Do not abide by the regulations and will find themselves in trouble. 'Why pay the B's, they wouldn't know what to do with the money.' Classic remark end of season.*

Each time we wrote a draft report, the contents were communicated to the management. Des invited discussion on practical and realistic improvements to camp sites, pay, food and so on. As with Wave Hill, some solutions were easy, but in many cases bluff and bluster on Des's part were all that could be done to improve conditions. The difficulty was in following up our recommendations and criticisms. Distances were long, resources were short, and the politics did not support us. The politically powerful cattle industry easily deflected criticism for mistreating Aboriginal workers, unless proof of truly barbaric and brutal treatment was forthcoming. In those days not paying wages to Aboriginals wasn't something that anyone other than us got too upset about.

We did change a lot. We were ensuring that workers were paid. At Wave Hill we got the wood brought in for their fires and latrines dug, which did a great deal for hygiene. We had some people sent to the Hooker Creek settlement, which helped them. We also knew that Rome wasn't built in a day, and that these were people who had endured several generations of serfdom. We had the power of the law and the southern press was beginning to take notice. By the 1960s, the big companies were starting to lose influence.

Of even greater concern was the mistreatment of part-coloured girls living about the drovers' plants. Full-blooded Aboriginals and part-Aboriginals did not always see themselves as one people, even if they had blood relatives. Part-coloured people often saw themselves a cut above their full-blooded cousins and half brothers. When young girls approached puberty, there was the prospect of them not having the protection of either culture.

These girls were not wards, nor did they always have a place in tribal society, so they often ended up in limbo, having to do the best they could in cattle stations and along the stock routes. Many part-Aboriginal and European stockmen had steady relationships with 'yella fella' girls, and raised their children in the stock camps with as much care and attention as the conditions permitted. Yet there were always exceptions who had to become our concern. The tribal husbands of the mothers of half-castes did not always recognise that child. Thus the child would have no protection nor be incorporated into the skin system. This did not stop such husbands from claiming a pretty girl at puberty in order to assert control for an economic reason.

Young part-coloured girls became playthings of the outback, to be used and swapped like currency. At the drovers' camps I sometimes caught a momentary glimpse of these girls, who were hidden away when our curiosity became obvious. They depended for their livelihood and safety on the whims of the men in the camps. Yella fella girls were talked of as 'studs', so that a girl may be known as 'Old Jack Riley's stud', for instance. Who would ever know they existed, let alone how they were treated, or what happened to their babies? There were many successful cases of part-coloured girls being removed for their own protection by the welfare authorities of the time.

Back in Darwin, some of my friends and occasionally the press were critical of the Welfare Branch taking away children. But what if the mother was barely out of puberty, with no way of independently looking after herself, let alone her child? What if the mother was under the influence of some dissolute itinerant stockman? Young girls were becoming mothers way before they were old enough to be good mothers, in conditions of unspeakable squalor and cruelty, often inflicted by the child's father – if he had bothered to hang around – but more likely at the hands of those in the Aboriginal community who had no truck with 'yella fellas'.

Granted, before my arrival in the Territory, full-blood Aboriginal children had been taken from the comfort and safety of their parents and from the culture of their tribal setting, for the purpose of their supposed better assimilation into our 'superior' way of life, or by misguided missionaries who sought to lead them from the way of the heathen, and on to the path of righteousness.

I knew a few of these children. One, by then a young man, lived with one of the well-known legal families, and seemed happy enough at first sight. In fact he was desperately lonely. He could read, write, and speak English fluently, and he wore clothes 'properly', yet there was no place where he fitted in Darwin society. To the disappointment of his adoptive parents, he returned to his own people near the Bagot settlement.

But not all cases were driven by well-meaning callousness. Our Department was instrumental, before my time in the Territory, in ending the taking away of children purely for ideological reasons. Ted Milliken, a trained psychologist, brought to our work a more structured overview to what had been developing since 1949.

That year Ted Evans was given a task that distressed him very much. He was, I understand, required to remove a number of part-coloured children from Wave Hill station. Sudden removal is bad enough but abruptly and by air even more so to people unused to aircraft.

Upon his return to Darwin, Ted wrote a summary report not to his superior, the Director of Native Affairs, but to the Government Secretary Reg Leydin, setting out his concerns about what had happened at Wave Hill. This prompted the Administrator, Mick Driver, to discourage all sudden and uncounselled separations, particularly by air.

Thereafter, patrol officers were asked to look out for part-coloured children who were not fully integrated into a family or tribal structure, and make a humanitarian assessment of the child's future. If the officer was experienced, he was to discuss the benefits of an education away from the camp with the mother and the child. If the officer was not experienced, a report (such as the one I filed from Wave Hill in 1957) would suffice to alert Darwin, and for someone in head office to take the matter up. Months would be allowed to elapse before a follow-up visit would be made by an experienced person from Darwin.

While the word 'counselling' was not used this was, in effect, what occurred. I never did follow up any cases myself as I was very much occupied with other matters, and I was certainly far from experienced. In effect, the patrol officer's job was to sow the seed in the mind of the child and mother and if there was any follow-up it was done over a period of time by experienced personnel.

Apparently there were instances where a mother and child had approached a patrol officer asking that the child be given a chance to 'better' himself. The story is told of a young boy called Mickey Cousins and his mother who made such a request to Ted Evans. Ted's approach was to allow the boy to accompany him for the remainder of his patrol and then to meet up with the mother at a predetermined spot, in this case the Negri races near Mistake Creek. All is reported to have gone well and Mickey went off with Ted to Darwin. There is no doubt that Ted in his own determined way brought about real changes. Perhaps when someone who knows more about these things than I writes a full history of the times, 1949, and Ted Evans at Wave Hill will be seen as something of a watershed.

Ted Milliken arrived to take up his appointment as Assistant Director of Welfare, directly under Harry Giese in October 1955. A slightly built man, he had been a naval lieutenant during the war, and while not a drinker, he still went out of his way to socialise with us all. My first sight of him captured the essence of the man's marvellous incongruity: there he was, in his very proper naval white shorts and shirt, but with bare feet, sitting on the floor of his room at the Mitchell Street Mess as we all had a drink to welcome him. Ted was knocking back soft drink.

On his drive up from Adelaide Ted had stopped at Tennant Creek to sit in on the Eva Downs court hearing. There had been allegations that native workers on the Eva Downs property had at times been flogged with stockwhips. A man, his wife and two others had fled from Eva Downs station. Two mounted stockmen gave chase and caught the workers near Anthony's Lagoon police station. From atop their horses, the stockmen meted out a severe flogging with their whips, inflicting particularly brutal cuts on the woman's chest. As chance would have it, a patrol officer saw the wounds and insisted on prosecution. The stockmen were found guilty at a criminal trial (and imprisoned) and damages were awarded to the Aboriginal workers in a subsequent civil trial. The civil action probably discouraged any more floggings. This was Ted's introduction to life in the north.

Coincidentally the Eva Downs court hearing must have been very close in time to Gordon Sweeney's and my investigation of the hobble chain flogging. Two incidents of this kind in the Australia of the 1950s, so close to each other, is indicative that we certainly had a job to do.

In 1957 Ted began putting together a set of guidelines for assessing whether a part-Aboriginal child should be removed from his or her own mother on a settlement or pastoral property. By 1959 these had evolved into their ultimate written form. However during all my time working in this area directions to me were verbal, possibly because I only made recommendations and did not have the task of actual removal.

The guidelines covered seven points, centring on the child's status within its community: if a male, was he likely to be initiated in due course; if a female, was she promised at birth to be the wife of a tribal male, and if not, was this because she was not accepted as part of the tribal group? Had the mother and the mother's brother already assumed that the child would be placed in a children's home? (It was often hard to know who a child's father was, so the uncle became the authoritative male figure.) Did the child live a full-blood lifestyle? Would the child be disadvantaged by entering a European school? Did the mother think the child would be better off?

The guidelines finished with the question: 'Having considered all points separately, is the child likely to live a more contented happy and fuller life, if removal occurs, than if he is left where he is?'

Despite what some critics might say now, this wasn't a leading question. Many children were assessed on these guidelines and were judged to be better off staying where they were. Many, also, were not. I never personally removed children, although I did recommend this. Never, however, were children taken from families with a mother and a father. They were *always* from very young and unprotected single mothers, often young girls between 10 and 13 with no family member to properly care for them. On the occasions that I recommended the removal of children from their families, it appeared that the alternatives were pretty shocking.

Friday June 14 1957: *Investigated complaint about a lubra and discovered a very dark coloured girl from Broome out at Tang's. Took her away and gave her to the care of the Bishop. Intend repatriating her to Broome.*

This young girl had been taken from Broome – willingly or otherwise – by Japanese pearlers on their lugger, who then dumped her in Darwin after the crew had no more use for her. Aboriginal girls were not too good at doing shipboard chores – they were used by the pearlers to satisfy their sexual urges. It was the Bishop who got me on to that case, and I have no doubt that in this case what I did was in the best interests of that young girl.

She was lost and without family, abandoned, used and without resources. What was the Welfare Branch to do for her? Her case was an extremely pointed illustration of a person who didn't belong anywhere. For the time being the only thing to do was to ask the nuns at Garden Point to take her.

On this occasion there was much debate in the Darwin press and Legislative Council concerning the authority of our department and that of the Director of Welfare, Mr Giese. I spent a considerable time assisting him with amendments to the Welfare Ordinance. It struck me that the wards of state set-up was universally disliked by the elected members of the Council, as well as a few appointed members, but the Federal Government was determined to persevere with this bizarre concept.

Then there was prostitution, particularly of part coloured girls. Aboriginal culture gave some protection to its women, but this could be brushed aside by the need for liquor. Part-coloured girls, not brought up with the protection of Aboriginal culture, faced the danger of being used by any passing stranger. Stockmen, fencing contractors, bore sinkers, station cooks and other itinerant single whitemen were desperately short of female company.

It was part of our duties to look into the care and protection of such girls, and as a consequence of this we sometimes recommended their removal. In November 1957, at Wave Hill, I wrote a report on six part-coloured children, three girls – all sisters – and three boys, that illustrates some of the issues we confronted when removing children.

Sheila was almost ten, and a possible candidate for adoption. I recommended against this as she was probably to old to fit into a white family. In my report I wrote: 'her social habit and behaviour is such that she is not even one step removed from the squalor of camp life as exists at Wave Hill. I do recommend, however, that she be removed as I consider there may still be time to improve this girl's social status. Garden Island or Croker Point would be the immediate solution. Finally, and this is common to all female part-coloureds, it has been noticed that girls a little older than Sheila become popular mistresses to both black and white persons in the outback, an argument greatly in favour of their removal to an institution'.

Pauline was eleven, and already tribally married. Again, I felt her young age put her at risk and argued that she also be sent to Garden Point or Croker Island, even though this was 'one of those border cases where it is difficult to judge whether or not removal is in the best interests for this girl's future and peace of mind'.

Jane, at five the youngest, was, I thought, a suitable case for adoption, 'if we could remove her from her present environment without too much suffering on the part of Jane or her mother'.

I was less inclined to recommend removal for the boys. 'I think in the case of part-coloured males removal is not as imperative as in the case of females,' I wrote. 'With the possibility of a school being opened at Wave Hill, I see no reason why Jimmy could not be educated there.' Five-year-old Jimmy, I thought, had good prospects ahead of him. 'Chaps of his position usually become good stockmen, sometimes owning their own droving plants.'

Jimmy's two-year-old brother, Barry, was the beneficiary of an understanding I was not, for some reason, apparently willing to extend to the girls. 'Barry at two years or possibly three now could well be adopted. If this child had been a girl I would possibly recommend it. In this case I am hesitant, as I often wonder if the pain of separation is worth it in a lad's case.' Like Jimmy, I assumed that Barry could go far with an education at Wave Hill.

As for ten-year-old Jock, he was best left where he was, I recommended, to serve his apprenticeship in stockwork.

Young, part-coloured boys' lives could go either way, as we saw it. They could forever be regarded as Aboriginal boys with all the incumbent problems and restrictions of that, or they could be raised as Europeans with all the benefits that entailed (voting, drinking, better education and jobs). When we found them, they were often at this 'crossroads'. When we sent them to hostels or schools their ties with their mother were not severed – that was never our intention. Our motivation was to give them a better chance at life.

I have no recollection now of the children referred to in this report. The girls may have been sent to Garden Point on Melville Island. This was not done on the spur of the moment. In many cases the mothers were taken and shown where their girls were being sent. Such separations were accompanied by much heartache and sorrow on the part of the children and their mothers, and we were not blind to this, but the child's welfare was a priority.

White children deemed 'to be in need of care and protection', or 'likely to lapse into a life of vice and crime', were similarly separated from their mothers, in Melbourne and Sydney. Indeed, there were white children removed who were living in conditions significantly better and safer than those in which we found Sheila, Pauline and Jane. The chances of those three girls leading wretched lives as part-time concubines for whoever was passing by, was very real. There was also a significant chance of serious injury if they became pregnant and were abandoned.

Choosing between adoption and removal, between leaving a child in a potentially dangerous situation and the trauma of separating a child from its mother, made decisions exceptionally difficult.

We also had to consider the stratified social fabric of the Territory. Part-coloureds like Babe Damaso lived like white people; others were condemned to abject poverty, something very close to slavery. A person brought up without the protection of a tribal life, without any supporting family other than a very young mother, who almost certainly had been abused since birth, was going to be kicked from arsehole to breakfast time.

These children were often the butt of cruelty not only from whites but also from full-blood Aboriginals. Brother Pye of the Catholic mission at Garden Point once saw a six-year-old part-coloured boy speared by a full-blooded Aboriginal, almost as a joke, just because the boy was a 'yella fella'. Brother Pye took this boy under his wing, probably saving his life.

Half-caste kids would now and again turn up at missions with spear marks and signs of horrific beltings. Babies were occasionally abandoned and young children left to fend for themselves. 'Yella fellas' could find themselves in a no-man's land and a no-win situation. No one will ever know how many were left to die, killed or simply pined away. It was part of my job to scout out potential tragedies.

Many of the children taken away were being given a chance to live and not die, to have a life beyond childhood without being permanently maimed. Garden Point, a mission set up in 1941 on the north-west corner of Melville Island, was a preferred destination for these children. By the early 1950s, the mission was a very important and integral piece of the welfare jigsaw. In 1941, thirty of the part-coloured children at Garden Point had Japanese fathers. One wonders if any of these fathers flew overhead to bomb Darwin later in the year.

> Thursday 12 September: *Office 0800. Some trouble at Batchelor so left to investigate. Appears as though there was a fight amongst the natives due to grog given by whitemen in exchange for women. One native was given one month in jail. Pity it is so difficult to convict white offenders. Arrived back in Darwin 2300.*

CHAPTER 11

My next assignment was to drive to Haasts Bluff, some 160 miles west of Alice Springs – at the end of an ungraded dirt track. Naturally, I looked upon this as another adventure, particularly as I was taking a new Land Rover with me. Haasts Bluff had originally been a government ration depot with the Hermannsburg Lutheran Mission attached. When I arrived there it was also the temporary headquarters of a superintendent destined to be in charge of the nearby Papunya settlement, which was then still under construction. As such it was run like a settlement, but was also being allowed to run down as all funds were being spent on Papunya.

I was to join up with Jerry Long at Haasts Bluff. He was planning to take a patrol into the areas around Lake Macdonald on the West Australia border in the hope of making contact with the Pintubi people.

The Pintubi could be found in lands straddling the Northern Territory and Western Australia border near lakes Macdonald and Mackay. A few of them had met up with Europeans, but others were thought to be some of the last uncontacted Aboriginals in Australia. One group, which walked into Haasts Bluff in December 1956, provided Jerry Long with details of their families still out in the Western Desert. Further contacts had been made by Jerry and Ted Evans the next year, while patrolling the Lake Mackay area. The Department now wanted us to find as many of the Pintubi as possible, assess their condition and ascertain their needs.

Haasts Bluff had started life to halt the eastward drift of people from the Western Desert into missions, cattle stations and Alice Springs. It had for many years been managed by a government employee, but the Lutheran missionaries, under the guidance of a truly remarkable man, Pastor Albrecht, also had considerable influence on its operations. The Lutherans had already established a commendable rapport with other desert Aboriginals, such as the Arunta (or Aranda) people, at their Hermannsburg mission on the Finke River, where the missionaries busied themselves translating the Bible and other religious works into the Arunta language. The missionaries felt it was very important to conduct church services and teach the Gospel to Aboriginals in their native tongues. One of the mission's most talented sons was Albert Namatjira.

By the mid 1950s the water supply at Haasts Bluff was proving inadequate, so a new settlement, Papunya, was being built to the north where there were good supplies of artesian water. The Papunya settlement was allocated all available funds, and the Haasts Bluff buildings and plant had become run down, ramshackle affairs. Jerry saw to it that most able-bodied men were put to repairing fences and bores, tending gardens, carrying out stock work or assisting the workforce constructing Papunya.

I was relegated to a galvanised-iron 'house' with Jerry and a school teacher, Bill Coburn, who had known my brother at teachers college in Melbourne. The floor of this house was concrete. The main room was a large farm kitchen with a fire stove. On the good side, like most pre-war outback houses, it boasted a large verandah with flywire walls. Here we congregated in the cool of the evening for a drink while preparing dinner.

As I wrote home: 'We kill our own beef here so we eat rather well. And Jerry insists on buying sherry and claret by the keg. (He's one for a pre-dinner sherry and claret with the meal – nothing too fancy, mind you.) We have one keg of each at the moment. I think that is what you should do at home. Claret by the keg works out at two bob a bottle and sherry much the same. So every evening meal we drink sherry when we are cooking then switch to claret while we are eating. Bang on what.'

At Haasts Bluff, as with all communities of Aboriginals kept on welfare, boredom and inactivity were serious problems. The Licensing Ordinance's prohibition of liquor, combined with the distance from Alice Springs, meant Haasts Bluff was spared frequent fighting and quarrelling. Nevertheless, it wasn't easy finding activities to stave off the boredom that welfare imposed in place of traditional ways. It was dispiriting to see grown men sitting in the dust playing marbles or laying around asleep among the corrugated iron sheds, surrounded by red dust barrenness and yelping mangy dogs.

The dog population was large, greedy and diseased. The Aboriginals in the camp didn't equate the sickness of the dogs with their ill-health. Jerry's idea was to shoot at least one dog per day, and often as we gathered on the verandah for a drink after work someone would ask, 'Have you shot your dog yet?'

The task wasn't easy. Whenever any of us was seen walking towards the camp with a rifle there was a flurry of dogs being hidden, in some cases under the dresses of the women. 'Himfella plenty good hunting dog boss, properly altogether good kangaroo dog, no shoot'em that one.' One look at the mangy, sick, limping animal would be enough to immediately see that even a rabbit could have had it for breakfast. This regular sniping didn't make much of an impression on numbers. Following an outbreak of scabies, the police were called in. Amid anguish and cries from the natives, the police slaughtered a large number of dogs, and dumped them in a mass grave.

Yet despite the worst aspects of Western lifestyle, the rites of initiation and reciting the songs of the Dreamtime continued.

Tuesday 8 October 1957: *Local holiday – anniversary of first sinking of bores. Church for troops in morning. Sports afternoon – a lot of work to organise. Considered barbecue lunch a suitable curtain raiser.*

> *Troops seemed to enjoy it. Spear throwing a disappointment, most definitely a weapon to be used within twenty yards. Entered one hundred yards race, didn't get a place. Firelighting competition for old men – very good flame within three minutes. Unlike Melville Islanders, shield and woomera being instruments for making fires.*

The son of the original Pastor, Paul Albrecht Jnr, was conducting church services in the old chapel and running a small canteen. Pastor Paul was a very friendly young man, ready to join in the functions Jerry would organise. One was a sports afternoon to celebrate the anniversary of the sinking of the bores at Haasts Bluff.

Pastor Paul won the spear throwing event and carried off the twenty pound bag of flour that served as both target and trophy. This was an unlikely skill for a Lutheran, but he admitted that most of his childhood friends had been Aboriginals, and they had taught him many of their traditional skills. 'I'm not too bad with a spear,' he joked, 'provided I'm close to the target and it's not moving.'

The spear, he said, was really used by Aboriginals as a stalking weapon. The main skill was to silently and unobtrusively position oneself near an animal, and strike from a fairly close distance. To achieve this, tracking, knowledge of animal instincts and the ability to move through the scrub undetected were essential. Lacking these skills, Pastor Paul said, he would have been placed last in the class.

There was a good sense of community. All the Europeans helped build a basketball court, which proved a successful and novel method for the young men to let off steam. Water was sufficient for a gardening project to produce enough vegetables for the workforce, pregnant women and children. Cattle projects, including maintenance and fence building, were always in need of workers. Jerry put a lot of effort into upgrading what passed for a kitchen, and trying to ensure camp hygiene did not fall below a very basic level.

> Sunday 13 October: 0830. *Noticed white fellows camped nearby – discovered they were dentists doing a survey on saliva acids of Aboriginal people. No permits to be on Haasts Bluff. Discovered from radio to Areyonga that they had permits for that settlement so all OK except for red tape which didn't seem important so let them carry on. Jerry arrived back and I left for Alice Springs. Arrived 1950. Drank on.*

In late October, Jerry, a mechanic, two trackers – Nosepeg and Tuppa Tuppa – and I left Haasts Bluff heading almost due west in search of the Pintubi. Most of the Pintubi had not made contact with Europeans, although they knew of our existence from having seen aeroplanes and from discussions they had with neighbouring tribes such as the Pitjantjatjara, from which our trackers Nosepeg and Tuppa Tuppa came.

One way of finding nomadic Aboriginals in the great spaces of the outback was to drive into their country and scout around for recent habitation, such as old fires, remains of food, excreta and the like. When something alerted Nosepeg we put up a 'smoke' by setting fire to the spinifex grass. This smoke was fairly dense and black, due to the oily content of the spinifex. If Pintubi were in the area and saw our smoke, Nosepeg said, they'd probably light an answering smoke, which we could then drive to.

Ted Evans and Jerry had used this technique to find some families of Pintubi in June. On that occasion, photographs had been taken of the people they'd met, and we had copies of these to show anyone we might meet up with on this journey. The June patrol, and the conversations Jerry had had with the Pintubi at Haasts Bluff who had come in a year earlier, provided us with a rough idea of the numbers and some names and family relationships we could encounter.

Our party was equipped with two new long wheel base Land Rovers and two trailers. The vehicles were specially fitted out with tanks along each side of the trays, one carrying water and the other fuel. Additional 44-gallon drums were also taken, together with spare wheels, tyres, radiators and so on. One of the problems of driving across the spinifex plains was the tendency for radiators to choke up with seeds, hence the spares.

Aerial photographs of the ground we were to cover had been pieced together into a map to assist us in pinpointing where we were at any one time. By radioing back to base twice each day we would – we hoped – be able to keep our whereabouts known in case of any emergency.

On the first day out we said goodbye to the last signs of civilisation at Tarawara bore at 8.30 a.m., and passed Petardi Hill (named by an earlier patrol) about midday. The temperature was just over 100 degrees Fahrenheit, so it was no fun when we bogged one of the vehicles in a sand dune that afternoon. Having two vehicles made getting out easier, but digging sand in the heat taught us to be more careful in the future. Late that evening we camped at Ilbilli waterhole, but could not find any water in the damp sand that was located between two rocks. It was pure heaven when the sun went down and the desert cooled enough for us to roll out our swags, have a drink of our tank water and a little to eat.

Early next morning we made our first radio contact and were very pleased with the reception. It was also satisfying to be able to pinpoint our position on the aerial photograph.

We continued on, past two dry waterholes, named Wilbia and Winbri by Nosepeg. In the desert Nosepeg had an unerring skill of finding waterholes or places that had the potential for being so. These were usually found in the crevices associated with rocky outcrops, often covered with rocks by Aboriginals to prevent them being disturbed and fouled by animals. Nosepeg and Tuppa Tuppa would scout around looking for recent signs of habitation, and often found remains of past camps – human excreta, animal bones, and the remains of old fires. Stones had been set in patterns by children playing with them.

By Thursday we were passing the Kintore Range, after spending some hours at Putja waterhole where we managed to make about seven buckets of warm dirty water. Even warm dirty water has its uses, as we discovered the following day when we had trouble with one of the radiators and had to exchange it with one of our spares. Boiling radiators were big users of water, so it was important for us get as much as we could from any waterholes that Nosepeg could find for us.

At some point on Friday, we estimated that we had reached the West Australian border and so we made camp early. Nosepeg suggested that we put up a smoke – great billows of oily spinifex smoke reached up some hundred or so feet. The terrain was flat, so it would have been seen for miles around, but no answering smoke was seen so we set about fixing the broken radiator and a punctured tyre.

> Saturday 2 November: *Broke camp about 0730 and carried on for about thirteen miles in a westerly direction. Passed one dry waterhole with signs of a recent camp. Put up smoke and pushed on to Tjibaroo. Saw a smoke in the south and made for it. About fifteen miles south we parked vehicles and Mr Long and guides walked some distance and found two natives whose wives and children had fled.*

Tuppa Tuppa had taken up his position on the roof of one of the stationary Land Rovers. After a half-hour had passed he was yelling and banging furiously on the roof.

'Boss, Boss, Mista Long! Might be'im smoke longa dat myall mob.'

The banging continued, and he jutted out his jaw, as bush natives did to indicate direction.

Tuppa Tuppa didn't have a great command of English so the ever-ready Nosepeg, always anxious to be in the limelight, was quickly up on the roof taking over.

'Smoke from blackfella Boss. Might be I now take you fellas all along proper way.'

To the south there was a faint haze. Jerry and I wouldn't have picked it. We all bundled into the Land Rovers, drove for about fifteen miles, and then stopped on Nosepeg's word.

John Williams and I were left behind, while Jerry, Nosepeg and Tuppa Tuppa followed a set of tracks, on foot, for half a mile. At the end of their search were two Aboriginal men, their women and children hiding in mulga scrub some hundred yards away. Tuppa Tuppa returned to fetch John and myself, and the three of us set off in the Land Rovers.

Eventually we arrived in the area where the people had been sighted. With Tuppa Tuppa's help we could just make out two men, blending into the mulga and spinifex. In the distance we could make out the women and children, running off. The white men they could just about cope with, but the Land Rovers were something else entirely. The two men, carrying spears and shields, stood their ground at the sight of the Land Rovers. Nosepeg kept up a conversation just in case, and soon it was obvious to the two that there was nothing to fear. Smiles broke out, and they then spoke freely and animatedly to Nosepeg and Tuppa Tuppa. The women and children stayed hidden.

Nosepeg was in his element showing the Pintubi his knowledge of whitemen's possessions. His first great hit came when he turned on a tap from the side of one of the Land Rovers and let go a flow of clear water. This impressed our new friends no end. The contrast between this source of water and the wretched waterhole they were relying upon was enormous. The Pintubi were absolutely dependent upon a supply of water that was down a hole several feet deep. I lent into this soak to see a small seepage of wet sand that made a cup full of water every ten minutes or so. A bird flew out while I was investigating, which didn't give me too much confidence.

Almost everything we had and did was of great interest to our new friends: tinned fruit juice, matches, the photos of other Pintubi that we had from earlier patrols and, most of all, our use of the radio to speak to Haasts Bluff.

I had a sense of foreboding. We were witnessing the end of the Pintubi's lifestyle uncontaminated by Western culture. We were happy that we had found them, and had achieved what we had set out to achieve, but there was also an understanding that for these people, life would never be the same again.

The men had smeared mud over their bodies, which had us puzzled. Nosepeg explained that this was done in the hope of making them less thirsty. I think he meant that it kept evaporation and sweat down, but I have no idea whether it worked.

Before dusk, Nosepeg took a rifle and with the two Pintubi men went looking for wallaby tracks. The well-honed tracking skills of the nomads quickly brought the three within rifle range of a kangaroo. After that, it was up to Nosepeg to finish the job. Kangaroo was 'number one tucker' that would normally have taken hours to track and kill with a spear, so there was excitement as the men arrived back at the camp with enough meat to last several days. That evening with the kangaroo cooking slowly on the fire, and plenty of clear, clean water was a night we will all remember.

Jerry, with his usual patience and determination, recorded all the names, skins and totems of the new wards and had their relationships roughly worked out with those found on the earlier patrols. He also had a better idea of who was still out in the desert. Through Nosepeg we told the Pintubi that we would be moving on the next day. One of the men asked if he could come with us, as he was keen to visit his mother who had been in the party that had travelled the December before to Haasts Bluff. After making sure none of the others minded we agreed, and gave him the 'whitefella' name of Guy. It was, after all, the fifth of November, Guy Fawkes Day. Trust Jerry!

Next morning we headed north-west in search of more natives. In the course of the trek, one of our trailers bogged in the sand and we were glad to make a waterhole known as Yumari. There was some good drinking water at this hole, which was a considerable relief as the temperature was consistently well above the century, and finding water for the radiators was now a continual problem with most of the holes dry or with barely enough water to make up a few cups full.

If we had gone out earlier in the year it might have been possible to follow up on information that Guy and his friend had told us about another family, but we were now in a season of hot weather, too hot to warrant any further attempts to carry on. In any event we believed that most of the Pintubi had now either been found or accounted for.

We turned back, travelling with the Kintore Range to our right and made it to Mt Liebig bore on 6 November. It was terrific fun to get in and swim in the large water tank. I'm not one for astrology, but as a Cancerian, I know the stuff of the desert explorers is not in my make-up: give me Melville Island any day! Syphoning water over Nosepeg and Guy while Tuppa Tuppa stood watching, was one of my life's highlights, sheer bliss in century-plus heat. Nosepeg had a lot of fun showing Guy how to use soap. What a strange thing it must have been for Guy to see so much water frittered away after the mean amounts he had been used to. I must admit, I wondered more about Guy's wonderment at having clean, untangled hair for possibly the first time in his life.

The few days in the desert created a bond between us all. Nosepeg loved to talk, and in the evenings, sitting on our swags, he'd take me for a bit of a joke.

'Plenty hot, not much'em water, might be by and by me leave'em you young whitefellas. Might be perish longa desert.'

There was only one answer to this: 'Me boss longa tucker box, might be no more 'em tin fruit.'

Tuppa Tuppa usually just grinned away – his command of English was almost non-existent.

The life of the desert nomad was very hard. The men, their wives and their four children depended on a very small water supply, in heat constantly well over the century, living off little lizards, a few seeds and anything else they could get their hands on. Yet the Pintubi had avoided 'civilisation' for so long thanks to their attachment to 'their country'.

Guy remained a few months at Haasts Bluff, enjoying the company of his mother. A national mapping team was then keen to visit Lake Macdonald and Jerry took Guy back to his family while escorting this team back over his old tracks. Some time later Guy walked all those two hundred miles, back through that hot desert, with his family to Haasts Bluff. The name Guy did not stick. He is now known as Timmy Tjapangarti and lives near the Kintore Ranges.

The eastward immigration of the Pintubi continued until bores were sunk at the Kintore Range in the late 1960s and early 1970s. These deterred their further drift, and encouraged a number of them to leave Haasts Bluff and Papunya to return and re-occupy 'their country', when it became clear that dense habitats were of less benefit than we'd hoped.

CHAPTER 12

Throughout 1957, I had kept on at the Department to allow me to use my pilot's licence in my work, but there was no luck on that front. To keep up my flying hours on the odd occasions that I was in Darwin, I needed an endorsement from the Department of Aviation to fly Tiger Moths, as they were the only aircraft that I could get hold of. Fortunately, I was able to put the flying to another use. After attending Mass one Sunday, I had met Mary McNamara, the acting chief pharmacist at the Darwin Hospital, who possessed great charm and liveliness. She had a sense of adventure, too, which she needed to agree to go out with me, not to mention flying in my Tiger Moth.

On my various trips to the hospital, I conjured up numerous excuses to visit the pharmacy – headaches, ingrown toenails, life-threatening illnesses – and after some fumbled attempts, eventually got around to asking her to the local flicks. It was arranged then – next Saturday, a film at the open-air picture theatre, followed by a few drinks. But first, a flight over Darwin. Her white-knuckled endurance of my early afternoon treat put my own picture of my flying abilities into perspective: oddly enough, she was to come up with me again a couple of times.

At Christmas I went down south to my family, friends and the Point Lonsdale surf. On the way down, I stopped off at Brisbane and enrolled as a correspondence law student at the University of Queensland, which accepted my ASOPA course as an adult matriculation. I felt in many ways that the stains on my academic slate had been wiped clean.

I'd been in and out of the courts as a patrol officer. I enjoyed watching counsel argue and had even had a dabble at it myself. As both patrol officers and welfare officers we had the right of audience before the courts when wards were involved. Mum and Dad thought that in choosing law, I was a little above myself, and my colleagues down south were surprised. The Welfare Branch saw it as ominous – some years later at Owen Dixon Chambers in Melbourne I ran into Mr Giese in the lifts. He jokingly said that he'd wasted a year's worth of Sydney on me.

Mary met me on my return to Darwin, and we celebrated with dinner at the flashiest spot in town, the Darwin Hotel. I picked her up at her quarters at the Darwin hospital at the appointed time, dressed in long white trousers, white shirt, and my Queensland University tie. I felt a million dollars.

Over the next few days I spent my free time building up flying hours with a couple of flights to Melville and Bathurst Islands, where I'd be met by the nuns bearing a jug of cold drink. Flying gives you an exhilarating sense of freedom, particularly when you're flying at five hundred feet (sometimes – stupidly – even lower). It is intriguing how a bird's eye view of country you know can so affect you. Flying in those days was far less formal than it is today. We didn't even have radios in the Tiger Moths I flew. As for navigational instruments, there was a compass, gauges for fuel, height, airspeed, oil pressure, revs per minute, and a piece of string on a screw as a slip and skid indicator. That was about it.

Flying within a short distance of Darwin could be done without any navigational skills anyway, simply by following the coast lines. The regulations no doubt dictated otherwise. But in the Territory, few worried about regulations, of any sort. And I didn't, as I cruised low over idyllic islands at eighty knots on those clear tropical days.

Social life in Darwin had fallen into a pattern. Ted Evans had a steady group of friends he met at the Darwin Club after work. There was the Church of England priest, Father Jones, who outdid us all with his love of beer and bawdy witticisms. As for his religious pursuits, he would cross-examine Mary and me on what was going on at the Catholic Cathedral, asking for translations out of the

Latin, so he could slip them into his own High Church service. Then there was the well-known prospector and later parliamentarian 'Tiger' Brennan who left no one in any doubt regarding his view of Aboriginals as inferiors. Ted Evans tried his damnedest to shift his thinking into the twentieth century, but after a while realised it was a lost cause.

The white Territorians clearly saw themselves as a ferocious breed: another club habitue was the popular and fearless lawyer 'Tiger' Lyons, ruddy-faced, red-headed and voluble, with an Irish temper. No judge could control him in court. Darwin's other great barrister was Ron Whitnall. Seeing myself as on the way to the Bar I would sit in at the courts whenever possible, and marvel at how these two could be at each other's throat in court yet have a beer and a laugh together at their club that night.

The Darwin European community was full of characters. One day I was summoned by an indignant Methodist clergyman who sought my assistance in an unlikely demarcation dispute. Apparently, Father Henschke of the Catholic Church had buried a native. The Methodist was sure the dead man had been one of his flock and wanted me to set things right. Short of disinterring the body, I didn't know what to do. So we drove over to Father Henschke's to discuss the matter. Father Henschke was a very tall grey-haired man, who spoke with a high-toned drawl. He was not given to wasting words. The Methodist churchman, on the other, was very correct, very small and a bit precious.

We strode up the cathedral path to the presbytery door. Out shuffled Father Henschke.

'You buried one of my natives,' said the Methodist.

'Yes,' said Father Henschke.

'Why did you bury my native?' asked the Methodist.

'Because he was dead,' said Father Henschke.

He was known for his brevity. One Sunday at Mass, his sermon went something like this:

'In the name of the Father and of the Son and of the Holy Ghost. Amen. It is the third Sunday after Pentecost. My dear brethren. You've got to be good. In the name of the Father and of the Son and of the Holy Ghost. Amen.'

The rest of the mass was delivered in staccato machine-gun Latin.

The Territorian attitude to authority was so relaxed as to be almost non-existent. A native friend of ours, Basil, who cleaned at the hospital, had found himself in trouble with the law, so I asked my legal friends how we could help keep the poor bugger out of jail.

'Easy,' they all said over their grogs, 'get Mary to go character witness and undertake to keep an eye on him and Sammy Dodds (the Stipendiary Magistrate) is sure to let him go.'

So Mary fronted up to court, went into the box and said all the right things, which were all half-truths, and Sammy let Basil go. The very next week, Mary and I were back at the Club asking all our legal friends the same question as before – Basil had already broken his bond.

'Ask for an adjournment,' they said.

Even with my rudimentary legal knowledge, I could see that an adjournment was just another way of postponing the inevitable. I couldn't see how it would help Basil.

'Ah,' said one, 'but you see Sammy's going on long service leave.'

We sought, and were granted, the adjournment. Sammy went on leave, and his replacement, who was on a junket from Canberra, had no wish to create any problems, and so Basil was reprieved.

Putting aside the natural privations of living in the outback, we were on a bloody good wicket. Our salaries were pretty good and I had the added advantage of picking up lucrative travelling allowances. These allowances were designed for city office workers down south who might be sent to another town and have to pay for their accommodation. I never had to spend money while away and was rewarded for having to spend less. Many in the Territory gained from this loophole in the regulations, and it was a hole no one seemed the slightest bit interested in plugging. Upon this happy financial position I built a little more with some reasonable wins on the stock exchange. I was even in a position to send a small amount to my parents to help my young brother, who was now a medical student.

A week or so after my return, I was sent out to Borroloola, south-east of Darwin just in from the coast and close to the Queensland border. I'd never heard of this place until I was given my orders, but it was legendary, thanks to its hermits, whom I was soon to meet.

Ted Egan and his wife Rae had been living in Borroloola for some time. I was being sent there to temporarily replace Ted, whose investigating skills were to be put to better use reporting on a potential site for a new settlement in Arnhem Land, around the area to become known as Maningrida. Rae and his children were to remain at the home they had set up in the old Borroloola police station, locally, and jokingly known as 'the Residency'.

Mary was not too pleased that I would be leaving. But then the Department informed me that I was required to take out a considerable quantity of pharmaceuticals to replenish Borroloola's stocks. Here was a great opportunity. If, let us say, the pharmaceuticals went missing, or could not be put together in time, then Mary would have to come out for a trip to Borroloola herself.

Well, the stores did go missing, and I went off to Borroloola, and then the stores were found, hidden under some Aboriginal artefacts in the hospital's native ward. Mary and a fellow conspirator had some explaining to do, and she didn't get to Borroloola anyway.

Borroloola was a short distance down the McArthur River from the Gulf of Carpentaria. The original township had its beginnings in the 1870s as a port and staging place for stockmen droving cattle from the Kimberleys. In those days there were no bores across the Barkly Tablelands, and stockmen had to follow the coastline of the Gulf country to water their cattle. The McArthur River provided an obvious place for cattle and the drovers to rest, particularly as it was near enough to the coast for stores and mail to be shipped from the eastern states. It was in these circumstances that Borroloola came into being. Drovers must have found the frontier town a most welcome relief, as it was a good 500 kilometres south-east of Katherine, the last town they would have seen and rested in.

The original settlement was a rough and tumble affair, at least until the police station was built in the mid-1880s. Many stories are told of the rogues, criminals and dropouts that once gravitated to Borroloola. The famous Bill Harney once did a stint in the cells at the police station, along with cattle duffers and the murderers of Chinese fossickers. The cell block had gone when I arrived, save for the concrete floor in the middle of which was still attached the ring bolt to which prisoners could be chained. As with many old Australian towns there had also been a fairly substantial Chinese population, now long since gone but having left their mark with a large number of mango trees planted in the 1880s.

By the time I arrived in Borroloola in January 1958, the old township had disappeared except for the remains of the old pub, a derelict store and the old police station, now the Egan family home.

Apart from myself and the Egans there were only four other Europeans. Most colourful of these was Roger Jose, a hermit of indeterminate age, who lived in an upside down water tank with his Aboriginal wife, Biddy.

Another old bloke, Jack Mullholland, lived alone in the crumbling ruins of what used to be Borroloola's last pub, which was appropriate given his fondness for drink. Jack, who had been in the Royal Navy, took over the pub's licence in 1945, but trade was not what it should have been and both the pub and Jack had since deteriorated.

For some reason this old pub was still on the mailing list of various magazines from Australia and abroad. These Jack stacked – unopened – in chronological order, not to gather dust, but for reading, later. Jack was in no hurry and in any event he was a slow reader. However, he wouldn't contemplate skipping a few months and getting himself up to date, so he was following events at least one year after they had happened.

Another antiquated reprobate whiled away the last of his days in an alcoholic haze under a crumbling mess of old galvanised iron that was once a store. God only knows what his name was.

Completing the Borroloola roll call was a lone missionary. This intense and excitable zealot was supported just below the poverty line by an equally earnest band of Christians in Sydney. Not that his intensity was a complete waste, as he spent his time single-handedly introducing literacy, numeracy and Christianity to as many of the Aboriginal children as he could entice to his makeshift school.

These outpost representatives of European superiority lived next to a really good bunch of Aboriginals. The contrast between those that were to be assimilated and the cultural role models was so marked that I now wonder why I didn't give up and return to Darwin on the next plane.

Mind you, the local Aboriginals could easily hold their own against us. They weren't buying the racial superiority business even if we did. One evening, while Rae Egan and I were having dinner on the verandah, I happened to look up and saw a huge snake slithering across the floor. Under normal circumstances, this would have turned my stomach, but in this instance, the snake was headed directly for her young baby, who was on a rug near the door. My natural cowardice evaporated, and I grabbed an old fighting stick, flayed into the snake's back and killed it.

Next morning I very proudly showed the dead snake to the men when they came up from the camp. They were less than impressed.

'Him not cheeky fella boss,' they smirked. 'Himfella something nothing.' Oh well bugger it. 'For me,' I thought, 'it was a bloody good effort anyway.'

Borroloola had been the one-time recipient of a large number of books donated by the American millionaire philanthropist Andrew Carnegie. These seemed somewhat out of place, unless one understood that for years, Borroloola's non-Aboriginal population had, as many old mining communities had, a hope for their future that the good times the mining or cattle industry gave them would go on forever.

These books provided the foundation for a library that was kept up for a few years until the town began to fall into ruins. The white ants ate what remained of the books after the moulding humidity of the tropics ruined them. Before the white ants had had their fill, however, Roger Jose read as many of the books as he could get his hands on. As a result, he could discuss any number of classical theorists from Plato to Descartes (which Roger pronounced Dezcartays). I thought I was pretty smart with my correspondence course in law, but Roger soon had my measure.

He would come down from his water tank to the Residency in the cool of the evening for a chat. I would usually offer him a chair but he always refused, saying he would prefer to sit on the floor. If offered a drink of beer he would again refuse. The first time he did this, I suspected teetotalism, but then he whispered: 'I wouldn't mind a small metho, though.'

Roger practised what he preached. What he preached was largely nonsense. Most days you'd see him coming down for water at our tap, wearing several layers of clothing topped off with a filthy old dressing gown. When I first saw this I was amazed.

'You must be boiling in all that,' I said. 'What's the idea?'

'No, Colin, all this clobber,' and here he grabbed a handful of clothes to show me just how much he had on, 'keeps me cool. If you leave an iron bar in the sun it gets hot, doesn't it?'

'Yes,' I agreed, wondering what on earth his point could be.

'But if you cover an iron bar it will stay cool. So must it not follow, that the more clothes you have on the cooler you will be?' Naturally, in the cool of the evening outer garments were taken off. He wouldn't have wanted to get cold.

I could have argued with him. I could have, but this was a man who wore as a hat an old ticking pillow case with one corner pushed in.

The ultimate was his footwear. Roger would turn up whenever I was killing a bullock, place his feet on the hide, cut off what he wanted and mould it to the size and shape of his feet. Then he'd take his bloodied feet out of the shaped leather and rub salt into his shoes to cure them. He used scraps of older leather as laces. His new moccasins always suited his needs.

We managed to always do the shooting close to a tree so we could throw a rope over a branch to pull the hind part of the bullock off the ground, using a vehicle to tow the rope. Then we would cut the bullock's throat, and once it had bled, half hanging from the tree, we would gut it, sever its head and then let it down from its half suspended position to skin it. That's when Roger would get his new footwear.

We didn't have a proper meat saw to halve and quarter it, so a blackfella would take to its back with an axe. Then the hacked-up bullock would be placed on its back, with its empty open carcass facing upwards. One of the experienced men would stand feet astride inside it while two others pulled the ribs apart. As neatly as he could, with a none too sharp axe he would cut down the backbone, halving the carcass. We'd then cut through at the second bottom rib to quarter it. The hardest trick was to preserve what one could of the eye fillet from the axe blows.

After the quarters had hung and set overnight Rae Egan and myself had the first choice. We would have the rump and porterhouse and whatever was left of the eye fillet. The rest was apportioned out. The white population who turned up got the round steak and the silverside. The blackfellas got all that was left over.

There were no electric refrigerators out in the bush. We used kerosene fridges, which often smoked and stank with the fumes, broke down and regularly sent the food off. We didn't plan on keeping the meat long. We shot a bullock each three weeks or so – I'm still not sure who owned them.

Outback life had turned Roger into a DIY expert, and under his guidance I had a go at making my own beer. He mixed two gallons of water, a handful of hops, three spoons of malt, three cups of sugar, and a few raisins and dried apricots for good measure. This would be brought to the boil, and allowed to cool before he added already-fermented yeast. The brew was then left for twelve hours, strained and then bottled with a pinch of sugar in each bottle. When the bottles stopped bubbling they were then corked.

In the first brew I made, many of the bottles blew up. Roger said this was because we had put the corks in too early.

'In case the others blow up as well, it would be a good idea if we drank them now,' he said.

He did. I had a couple of mouthfuls but it was warm and vile, so I settled for a Carlton Draught. My next attempt didn't turn out much better, so Roger had another windfall. While he was drinking this concoction, Roger confessed that he had once served six months in 'the Peter', as he called it, for peddling his brew to the Blacks.

Life in the Peter, said Roger, wasn't all that bad. 'The roof didn't leak, you got three meals a day that weren't bloody wallaby; in fact it was a home away from the bloody water tank.'

It is impossible to exaggerate about Roger. However I have always met resistance from listeners when I describe Roger's wife, Biddy. Biddy was so fat that she could hardly walk. That is where the wheelbarrow came in. If the two went out together, Biddy was to be seen sitting with her legs suspended over the front of the barrow, with Roger pushing her along, in his dressing gown and pillow ticking headgear.

The missionary spent his time serving his flock, with nothing but the meagre resources that irregularly dribbled in from his associates in Sydney. I discovered that he was living on two meals a day consisting of a form of porridge. It was no skin off my nose to ensure he was properly fed and provided with fresh meat and other food from government stores, given that he was providing the rudiments of an education to the local children.

I became intrigued with his efforts and asked whether I could inspect some of the children's work. He was more than happy to show me their work, and there was no doubt that he had taught them to read and write English, but all their efforts were devoted to copying holy writ.

It seemed to me that it might not be a bad idea to see how well they could perform, writing about non-religious matters, and so, with the agreement of the missionary, I invited all those interested to write a story on the events of their last sports day. About a dozen children presented me with their efforts. One fourteen-year-old girl wrote about a spear-throwing competition in which the men attempted to spear a twenty pound bag of flour, similar to the contest won by Pastor Albrecht at Haasts Bluff.

> *All the men from the camp they come*
> *to the top to the sides they throw*
> *but nobody they get*
> *then Pharo from the camp he come*
> *and Pharo he got.*

My daily routine at Borroloola involved keeping an up-to-date census for the Register of Wards, employing as many people as I could building a new Nissen hut, tending a fairly good vegetable garden, watching over a small herd of beef cattle, that I assumed was ours but was not sure, and carrying out some basic hygiene and medical supervision.

I also had to use the battery-operated radio at least twice each day to send off the weather report to the bureau in Darwin. For this I was paid ten shillings a week, with an extra fifteen shillings a week for maintaining the airstrip. The radio was our vital link with the outside world, not only for medical advice, but to place orders for goods to be sent out on the fortnightly plane and to send in reports, pay sheets and other records to Darwin. In the time I was there I worked my way up to bare proficiency at fiddling with the troublesome object, thankful only that it had superseded the previous model, which was pedal-powered. If I reached the weather bureau at first attempt I was thankful: generally I'd find myself speaking to all manner of persons, from aircraft personnel to stations in the vicinity of Cloncurry. One time I made contact with a ship.

It was also one of my jobs to give first aid and medical treatment to the local Aboriginals. It was a significant part of the job: people did have accidents, and although we had a radio, it was the wet season so nobody could come out except by air. Which meant that I had to play doctor. I'd been trained in giving injections at the Darwin Hospital – intramuscular, not intravenous, which were given by doctors and nurses. So I'd jab into a muscle and squirt in the penicillin, once I'd been given the OK over the radio.

Towards the end of my three-month stay, near the close of the wet season in March, I was kept busy organising young men to work as labourers for the Barkly Tableland cattle stations. The Borroloola men were much sought after as stockmen and fencers. One enterprising fellow – quite a hand at sinking and repairing bores – acquired an old army truck, in which he intended to head off as soon as the weather permitted. His ambition, to ultimately do this work on a contract basis was in those days unique, yet the Borroloola men were the most enterprising Aboriginals that I had dealings with, as enterprising as the Tiwis of Melville Island were amiable.

A week or so before I left Borroloola a murder occurred directly as a result of a breach of tribal law. Bill, a Yagamari skin, was killed by Leo Yulungudi, a Janama skin. Leo had a wife, Jessie, and a sister-in-law, Dulcie Limundu, who were each 'proper straight' for him (being of the Nurulama skin).

As things sometimes happen, Bill had been 'sweethearting along Dulcie'. In so doing, Bill had broken two tribal laws. He was guilty of 'humbuging' by breaking the skin laws. And he had stolen a girl promised to Leo.

Leo had no choice but to challenge Bill to a fight. This occurred at an agreed spot and Leo wasted no chances. He smashed Bill's skull with the heavy, hardwood fighting stick, and then fled the whiteman's law.

Leo was soon caught and charged and pleaded guilty to murder. On his plea the well-known Tiger Lyons represented him. The defence asked me to prepare a report and to appear in court as a defence witness to explain the implications of tribal law. Justice Kriewalt accepted Leo's difficult position in trying to abide by two different set of laws and sentenced Leo to six months jail for murder.

The fortnightly aircraft duly arrived and this time it was my turn to go. The good citizens of Borroloola all turned up to help unload the cargo – their pension cheque 'receipts'. Their pensions had been metamorphosed into the grog now being lovingly cradled in the arms of Roger, Jack and the other alcohol-soaked pensioner, whose name I never did find out. After boarding the Drover, with the unusual feature of three engines – one on each wing and one in the middle – I was again airborne and heading for Darwin.

CHAPTER 13

Back in Darwin there had been some changes. Mary had dropped out of my life. There'd been no drama, it had just faded away as young romances do. But there were lots of other people I was keen to catch up with. My old boss, Alan Pitts from Beswick, was now married and was the Superintendent of Bagot Settlement. Paul Ingram had been transferred to Delissaville, just across Darwin Harbour, and I was made town patrol officer, Darwin.

Paul and Tessa were one of those gregarious couples able to attract a group of people and turn the whole thing into a party. There was a plan to develop Delissaville into some sort of auxiliary settlement to Bagot. It was close enough (because it was half a day's drive away) but far enough to stop people walking into Darwin.

Within weeks I was asked to go across and help my old mentor draw up a detailed map of the various areas and creeks that might be useful for projects in which to employ wards.

I flew over the harbour in about fifteen minutes; to go around by road would have been the better part of a day. I had privately reached an agreement with the aero club to keep the Tiger Moth for two or three days.

When I landed at Delissaville, Jack Murray was already there with, of all people, Bill Harney (Billarni to the Aboriginals). Bill was a bit of a rogue, a bloke who could talk his way out of anything. He had written a few books including *Songs of the Songmen*. I had met him in Sydney when he was returning from having given some television interviews in London. More recently Bill had been 'sitting down' at Two Fella Creek, doing what he did best, lazing away enjoying the bush in the company of his friends the Aboriginals. Jack Murray had just dropped in some fuel for him and they had decided on the spur of the moment to sail up the few miles to see Paul and Tessa.

Coincidentally, an officer and sergeant from the RAAF base some twenty or so miles away had dropped in on the day of my arrival to ask Paul for some boys to help them on a bush turkey shoot. Paul and Tess were immediately in a party mood. The boys did shoot and dress some turkeys, Murray's boy was dispatched to catch some barramundi and the sergeant doubled back quickly to the Base to bring in some grog. What a great couple of days. Perhaps the only trouble was Billarni monopolising the conversation. But just for a day or so we could put up with that.

Paul and I were supposed to be driving around doing our survey thing noting timber stands, sandy areas, and likely areas for garden projects. It looked like an impossible task until the RAAF bloke suggested we use my aircraft. Throttle set, contact, the sergeant swung the prop, the Tiger Moth spluttered into action. We accomplished in an hour or so what would otherwise have taken days. A great party was had by all.

Sadly it was shortly after this happy event that Paul's gambling caught up with him and he was sentenced to six months in Fannie Bay. (Paul had taken a rather unorthodox approach to settlement bookkeeping and had been using the funds to pay off his racing debts.)

I returned to Darwin in early April after three days in Delissaville. The wet season had now gone and with its passing we had beautiful dry weather, glorious blue skies, temperatures around thirty degrees – and the races. Darwin didn't have many race meetings, but the one or two allowed people like Paul to bet on the southern races.

The Darwin race track was a very ordinary affair, an excuse for local men to drink and gamble. The one time I went, there were two races, each with only three or four horses cantering around the course. No one was watching. Not being a racing man I couldn't see the point of it all, until someone explained that it was purely a social event set up so the bookies could openly bet on the southern races.

My workload as town patrol officer was no longer novel and I liaised easily with the police, the hospital, the churches and most of the employers of native labour. I also knew more about the transient population of natives coming in from the surrounding areas. Driving around the town I would now be regularly greeted by Aboriginals who knew me, just as Ted Evans had been when I first arrived two and a half years before, and with whom I was beginning to build a rapport.

I would be settled here for at least a couple of months, and this helped my studies. The local magistrate gave me a hand on the law subject, and I studied each day before I left the office. During the day I would patrol in my government Land Rover, which I was also allowed to use for private business.

I was not bound by strict working hours which cut both ways: I could, and would, be called upon at all hours, including the middle of the night and weekends; on the other hand, I also took time off during the day to go swimming or fishing if I was out near a tempting patch of water.

When it came to work, my day was often made up of dealing with fights and injuries (particularly women being belted by their men), drunken natives, police, courts, churches, harsh employers, caring employers interfering in tribal custom, sickness, natives in transit, white men consorting with native women, and clashes between nomads and the whiteman.

Before coming to the Territory I had never seen anyone affected with leprosy. At East Arm, a peninsula jutting out into the Darwin harbour, there was a leprosarium conducted by the nuns. One of my duties was to visit that establishment as most of its inmates were also my charges. During my time in Darwin I took about half a dozen people diagnosed with leprosy to East Arm. The doctors and nuns had told and shown me what to look out for as possible symptoms of this horrible disease. One of the signs, easy to see on Aboriginals, was white blotches. I learned that contrary to popular belief, the disease was not highly contagious in a society that has good hygiene, yet whenever I had to assist I wasn't comfortable until I had gone home and had a thorough shower.

The leprosarium nuns were marvellous and the general morale was excellent. If caught early, and with good treatment, physical deterioration could be arrested. However, there were always people limping about on crutches displaying stumps of legs or with hands missing fingers.

Tuberculosis was another problem. I was always on the look out for this as I toured about the makeshift camps of the itinerant myall natives on Darwin's outskirts. Primitive people unused to hospitals and doctors sometimes hid their sick people, so I would routinely look inside the humpies. One day, looking past some not-too-willing residents I spied a bundle of rags lying in a huddle in the dark smoky dwelling. It was a young man, looking very ill. After some discussion with his friends and family I carried him in my arms, as he was very light, to my vehicle and then drove as quickly as I could to the hospital. He died in my arms as I was walking through the hospital doors. The doctor told me he had advanced TB and there was nothing else I could have done.

I was left with the problem of consoling his relatives, who were 'yakaiing' (wailing and cutting themselves in their customary manner of grieving), and without doubt blaming me for taking the youth away. As with all such removals to hospital I had some of his relatives accompany me, so at least they were with me at the time of death. It was normal in the native ward for many relatives to be camping about close to their sick family member.

By June I had a routine that gave me enough opportunities to get out into the bush, yet also allowed me to keep a steady room at the mess, and a desk at the office. There were social functions at the Darwin club, the nurses' home, the various service messes and the home of Alan Pitts out at the Bagot reserve. For the first time since arriving in the Territory, I was settled. It was then I was transferred to Alice Springs.

Alice Springs in the middle of winter is a very cold place, particularly in the evenings, when jumpers and long trousers are essential. Sitting in front of a log fire in the old Alice Springs hotel was a chilly reminder of the extremes to be found within the one Territory.

The town mess in Alice was a much smaller affair than those in Darwin. It catered for about seventy public servants of all sorts: lawyers, police, clerks, engineers, and so on. The fellow in the room next to me was a laboratory technician, and the one on the other side was a prison warder.

My boss, District Welfare Officer Bill McCoy, was a diminutive old man in a job that was, I think, beyond his capabilities. It was said of Bill that all he had above his shoulders was his ever-present pipe.

Bill's patch covered a vast area from the South Australian border in the south to Tennant Creek in the north. Aranda, Wailbri, Pitjantjatjara, Pintubi and Warramunga were the major languages. The gnome-like DWO supervised several settlements, missions, and the affairs of several thousand Aboriginals. Two hundred and fifty kilometres to the west was Papunya. To the south-west was Pastor Albrecht's Lutheran Mission of Hermannsburg.

The Catholics also had a mission to the south east, Santa Therese's. The priest in charge, Father O'Brien, was an Assumption College old boy, and in my time had been remembered as a great football hero, first XVIII. It was not all that unlikely in those days for an old boy priest from Assumption to have been good at football. His footballing nickname was 'Killer'. Father O'Brien ran the mission with much the same determination as he'd played football. Bill McCoy was always in a dither when up against either Pastor Albrecht or 'Killer' O'Brien.

At times I felt sorry for Bill, particularly as the Alice was a place many overseas dignitaries wanted to visit. Bill was the official such personages first contacted on arriving in Alice Springs. Their assumptions on the romance of central Australia were quickly dashed upon meeting Bill: five foot four, bland face, bland character, brown cardigan. This was no Chips Rafferty, rolling a fag in the saddle. (Although on reflection I met that film star in the Alice and also at one of the settlements and I'm sure I would prefer being stuck in the bush with Bill than the cardboard cut out. I once watched Chips refuse a tailor-made cigarette from a bushman, because he thought it wasn't what a real bush bloke would smoke! He talked a good game but I don't think he really knew anything about life in the bush.)

Our visitors were continually taken aback by the size of the place, and its individual laid-back style. One time I travelled out to Haasts Bluff and Papunya with Bill Bates, a senior officer from the British High Commission in Canberra. This trip required us to travel the 300 kilometres on a dirt track, much of which was ungraded and badly rutted. I had indicated to Bill Bates that it was good etiquette to take some hospitality with us.

'Quite what do you mean?' asked this charming and erudite Englishman.

'Grog,' said I.

He bought a goodly quantity of appropriate liquid rations and we set off. Our first stop was at Narwietooma Station, which was owned by a millionaire airline tycoon named Connellan. As we approached Connellan's homestead, a baffled look crossed Bates' face.

'Why, it's nothing more than a tin shed,' he exclaimed, 'but I say, is that not a Rolls-Royce over there?' There was a pause. 'In fact, I'll be damned, not one but indeed two Rolls-Royces – just left out there in the open, do you see Macleod?'

I could only agree, adding that beside the cars was the owner's private plane, neatly tied down.

'My God,' was all he could get out, before we were taken inside and given a cool drink. He certainly needed the drink once inside, when he was told that the older Rolls-Royce was used as a ute to cart about all manner of station items, from fencing tools to rolls of barbed wire.

As we were driving away from Narwietooma, there was some thumping on the roof of our vehicle. Sam, our tracker, was signalling us to stop. I pointed out a number of kangaroos.

'I say, Colin,' Bill ventured. 'Would you mind greatly if I had the use of your armoury?'

He then very professionally shot one of the 'roos. As he strode out to recover his quarry, I heard him remark to himself: 'Marvellous. Absolutely bloody marvellous.'

When we reached Haasts Bluff, my friend was all politeness and decorum as he was shown around the place. Dinner was cooked by Bill Dunn, a stockman used to bushman's fare. Dunn carried on a treat as he carved up huge pieces of steak, cut up the spuds and onions, and kept his throat well lubricated with grog. Meanwhile, he and a couple of his mates rendered the polite Englishman all but speechless with yarns and general conversation expressed in the very best of outback Australian vernacular.

As the meal progressed we all got stuck into the liquid hospitality the overseas visitor had generously provided. By dinner's end Bill Bates was standing on the table reciting ribald poetry, when all of a sudden he laughed and yelled out: 'Fuck, Fuck, Fuck! Every second word we say is Fuck!'

Another remarkable Englishman and journalist was attached to me while he made a film, *The Question for Johnny*, which was about the future of a hypothetical Aboriginal boy. We travelled east of Alice Springs to visit the Harts Range races. The venue was dry, hot and dusty, but the race meeting was fun, and there he met an English girl, the daughter of a verger. He fell seriously in love with her, and I believe they were later married. In any event, back in Alice he used my office and composed an ode to his new lady, which began;

Twas at the Harts Range races
Where the creeks don't run with water
There I spied the verger's daughter.

On another occasion he bounced into my room at the mess, and seeing *A Tale of Two Cities* grabbed it off the shelf, enthusiastically declaring that his very favourite sentence was in that book. He then read it to me, but before I remembered to mark it I had forgotten it.

I had a soft spot for the Poms perambulating through the Territory. They had a great sense of humour, and, in spite of their reputation, were unassuming and very witty.

Besides the roving Poms we also had to look after the anthropologists who were always on the prowl. If possible I took them out to Haasts Bluff and left them to the tender mercies of Nosepeg. One, from the Australian National University, brought with him some photos of rocks all laid out in a circle. These were similar to rock formations Jerry, Nosepeg and I had seen during the Lake Macdonald patrol.

The anthropologist was discussing these rock patterns and fell into the mistake of asking Nosepeg leading questions (like the anthropologist had when quizzing Ali about the grave poles on Melville Island). The way the questions were going I thought Nosepeg would lead him along about 'spirits' and the 'Dreamtime'. But no. He just looked up at the interrogator and said, 'Might be 'em all bullshit boss, them just all the time kids muck about, play games.' The look of disappointment on the visitor's faced was quite marked as he put away his photos. Nosepeg's eyes twinkled.

The Aboriginal population in Alice Springs was more noticeable and stood in stark contrast to the town's white inhabitants, even more so than in Darwin. The dry Todd River bed was the daily scene of poverty and indolence, with Aboriginals sitting and lying about. Anyone who worked with the people there knew this shocking sight was not of the Aboriginals' making, but rather the result of 'progress'. Still, impressions lasted.

It was here I met Albert Namatjira and saw at first hand how alcohol and the Welfare Ordinance combined to wreck this great Australian's life. Albert had a supposed favoured status: as a full-blood Aboriginal who was not on the Register of Wards, he could legally drink alcohol, yet this loophole was cruel and insensitive, as legally he could not enjoy a drink with his family and friends.

Albert was very much a presence in the town, driving or being driven in his own vehicle, much to the chagrin of many whites, especially those in the police force. Plenty of whites thought it was wrong for an Aboriginal to have a car and more money than them. The police on the beat were used to treating Aboriginals as if they had no rights at all. Police frustration at Albert's practical immunity was sometimes taken out on his sons and relatives. Arresting a 'Namatjira' was attended by not a little bombast among police on the street.

The inevitable occurred. There was no way Albert could avoid buying liquor for his own family, and he regularly exposed himself to the possibility of prosecution. Only the actions of certain corrupt police, who 'protected' him in exchange for paintings, kept him out of the courts. Ultimately, however, he was charged and convicted after buying his family liquor, and sentenced to jail.

On one shocking occasion, excessive drinking by young men in Albert's circle led to the brutal murder of a young Aboriginal woman near Morris soak, which was one of Albert's camps. I was with Jim Lemaire, the magistrate and coroner at the Alice, when he inspected her body, naked and bloodied on the red sandy soil, amongst the Mitchell grass and spinifex, her head smashed in at the back with a fighting stick.

The prime suspect was well known to all present as one of Albert's extended clan. Albert had been at Jay Creek at the time so he wasn't included in the coronial inquest, but when later I spoke to him about the incident, his eyes glazed over with sadness. I am sure even now that this tragedy hastened his death the following year, 1959.

From past experiences, it was likely that the murderer had been drinking methylated spirits coloured with tan boot polish to look like wine. As liquor was banned, the exploitation of Aboriginals knew no bounds. In their drive for higher profits liquor sellers didn't even supply the real thing. The dilemma was deciding whether or not to legalise liquor and so eliminate the supplier, in the hope that normal policing of drunkenness would suffice, or retain the evils associated with prohibition, and have 'bloody Abos' rolling around drunk and fighting everywhere. I suspect there is no answer that will avoid hardship, and I note that since the consumption of liquor has been legalised, some Aboriginal communities have restricted its sale and consumption within their communal boundaries.

The most outspoken defender of Aboriginal people was the redoubtable Miss Olive Muriel Pink. Miss Pink was in a class with Roger Jose, Jock McKay and Jack Mulholland when it came to Territory eccentrics. She had studied anthropology at Sydney University under

Professor Elkin, and on arrival in the north had appointed herself the protector of Aboriginals. She had two outfits. Winter saw the navy blue box-pleated skirt, long-sleeved white blouse, navy blue jacket and blue beret. Summer saw the off-white box-pleated skirt, long sleeved white blouse, and white pith helmet. She was straight out of the Raj.

Billy McCoy's office, along with those of Magistrate Lemaire, and the police inspector, were the main destinations for Miss Pink's forays into town. Fortunately for me my office was at the other end of town to McCoy's, in an old shop with large windows. It was, in fact, closer to Miss Pink's house, which meant that if I was in between nine and ten in the morning, I would see her scuttling past on her latest mission.

It took a couple of months before she realised that I was a port of call on her daily voyage up Todd Street, but by then I was well apprised of her resolve to set to rights, within the space of her own lifetime, all the evils perpetrated upon the Aboriginal race since 1788. My method of dealing with her was simple. If I saw her hesitating near the front door, I would duck out the back.

But there was no such retreat for the hapless McCoy. His office was a room from which there was no escape. For a time he tried to coincide his morning toilet break with her anticipated visit, but he mixed his times up too often. Out would come her little notebook of haranguing points, detailing the misfortunes she had seen befall natives about Alice Springs. Woebetide Billy if she arrived before his toilet break.

Miss Pink was a prolific letter writer to the Minister in Canberra, to the press and all officialdom. In Canberra and Darwin there were files, many inches thick, specially allotted to her correspondence. Not all of her letters concerned the plight of the Aboriginals. One famous letter to the Department of Civil Aviation complained that the planes were flying low over her house to spy upon her in her uncovered outside shower.

Not even the magistrate was safe. His Worship once threatened to jail Miss Pink for contempt. A young Aboriginal woman was in court charged and convicted of 'Abo drinking liquor'. She also had been given quite a beating by some part-coloured men. Miss Pink took up the cudgels on the young woman's behalf, abusing the bench for 'the injustice' of this girl being first cruelly treated by tormentors, who had escaped, yet then being convicted for drinking liquor.

She had a point, but her manner of expressing it left a great deal to be desired. No amount of gentle persuasion from the bench could induce her to cease her tirade of invective, and so the court had little alternative than to charge Miss Pink with contempt and have the matter stood down until later in the morning's court list.

The sergeant watch-house keeper, in whose custody she now looked like being committed, took fright at her wrath. In a brainwave, he rang up the jail governor and told him that Miss Pink was on her way, as an inmate. Within minutes the governor was at the court house, demanding an audience with the magistrate.

The governor's message was a simple one. 'You can sentence her all you like but she's not coming to my jail.'

By this time Miss Pink had walked out of the police station and was back at the court. The police prosecutor, a bull-necked, overweight, one-time boxer quickly moved that the daily court list be brought to an end. 'The remaining matters cannot proceed as there are no witnesses,' he rushed out. 'Would your worship therefore mind standing the balance of the list down to dates to be fixed?' To the relief of all, the court rose early that day, and Miss Pink's citation for contempt was forgotten. That day the Alice Springs Club had a few extra for lunch, with well-deserved drinks shouted by all.

Miss Pink's knowledge of the local Aboriginals and their movements was uncanny, but her special interest was in children, especially those part-coloured children in a Church of England hostel near her home. A Church of England welfare worker, Sister Eileen Heath, a lady of great patience and kindness, had her office in my building. Even she fled when the indomitable Miss Pink loomed into view. Despite her reluctance to engage Miss Pink in conversation, she was one of just two people in the Alice who was able to talk Miss Pink down. The other was the magnificent Matron Olive O'Keefe (a sister in law to Ron Ryan, the District Welfare Officer of Katherine) who was in charge of the native wing of the base hospital. Olive Pink had no hope against her, which meant that the hospital was the only place in the Alice free of her scrutiny.

Nowadays one could scarcely believe that Aboriginals were housed separately from others in the hospital, but they were, and for good reason. There was no other way for the hospital to function properly. If a child or an old person was sick, family members refused to be separated, which was understandable. The hospital adopted a very liberal approach to relatives camping in the grounds adjacent to the relevant ward. The reality was that to sanitise the area to the standards expected of a modern hospital had seen patients abscond in the past. Many would not even seek treatment. The native ward was an environment that recognised families' needs and cultural concerns long before the wider community did.

Nothing was too much trouble for Matron O'Keefe. Everything was done with a smile, tenderness and a considerable knowledge of tribal culture. There are many instances in tribal society where certain persons cannot see or look at each other, or even say each other's name. This meant that it was far better for patients and their relatives to arrange themselves, in some cases with patients actually camping out on the verandahs and grounds, eating the food of their choice, sitting around in groups on the ground or floors.

Not that Matron O'Keefe would tolerate any low standards. This great lady had the knack of keeping all the essential utilities clean and ordered as well as a reasonable discipline among her charges. Her care for all patients was such that she was later awarded an MBE.

My days were now so full, what with work, socialising and flying, that I had to discipline myself to ensure that I kept up with my university assignments. There was no flying club to borrow aircraft from, but there was a gliding club. I had a go, but never attained sufficient proficiency to go solo. The mess and the Alice Springs Club provided most of my spare-time entertainment, and there was a good flow of tourists to amuse me.

Mary had stayed in Darwin, and except for a month we were to spend together in Melbourne the next year, our paths didn't cross again. We were young, and distance had accelerated our drift apart. I was too young to even consider the idea of commitment.

The months rolled by and it was soon time to sit for my exams. The exam venue chosen by the university was the Church of England's parson's house. This was indeed good luck. The parson appointed his kindly and considerate wife as my overseer, and she ensured I wasn't to be flustered through the ordeal by providing me with cups of tea and home-baked scones. Naturally, time was added on for that lost in taking refreshments.

As the year neared its end, I felt that my time up north was coming to a close. I had applied for a year's leave of absence in the event that I passed my exams so that I could do the next year's study full-time, but this was refused, so I determined to resign if I passed sufficient subjects. In anticipation of success, I applied for residency in the Catholic colleges at Queensland and Melbourne universities, with Bishop O'Loughlin of Darwin as my referee.

I passed with honours in a couple of subjects, and I was accepted into Melbourne's Newman College for

1959. Fortunately my savings had grown, the stock exchange had been kind and there was the easily acquired Commonwealth scholarship allowance of £365 a year irrespective if one worked as well.

After many drinking sessions and multitudinous farewells I boarded the Ghan, as the Alice to Adelaide train was known. I was ordered to assist a Northern Territory policeman who was escorting a mentally defective prisoner to Adelaide. (I didn't formally resign until I got to Newman College, so officially I was still a patrol officer on duty.) It seemed to both of us that the prisoner was OK, and we took the risk of leaving his handcuffs off and shouting him a beer at a couple of the stops. After all, there was nowhere much he could run to.

The Ghan might not have had square wheels; nevertheless, they certainly were not round. The speed was slow, the food was awful and the train shook and jolted. Two of the three of us were very glad to detrain at Adelaide and go our separate ways: the prisoner into custody, the policeman to a mate, and myself to a uni student I had met in Alice Springs, who informed me she had a party for us to go to in the Adelaide hills that evening. I was keen to know what university life held in store.

CHAPTER 14

In 1983 and 1995, I revisited Bathurst and Melville islands. I was surprised at the large number of non-Aboriginals working there, compared to 1957, in spite of a supposed 'independence'. I wasn't there long enough either time to make informed judgments on what I saw, but on both occasions I was struck by the lack of dug-out canoes on one hand, and the plentiful supply of bread, fish and vegetables, imported from Darwin and paid for with welfare cheques, on the other. I also noticed that both islands boasted an Alcoholics Anonymous group and women's groups to help deal with domestic violence.

Bathurst Island Mission and Snake Bay are now known by their Tiwi names Ngui and Millicapiti. In 1995 I spoke at length to Brother Pye, who has been in the Territory working with Aboriginals since 1941, and is the custodian of some very interesting documents, the writer of informative articles and the possessor of a keen mind and memory. This dedicated and venerable gentleman laments much of the criticism levelled at the brothers, priests and nuns who ran the Garden Point mission for part-Aboriginal children on Melville Island.

He felt that in many cases these children were saved from real danger and abject misery by being sent to Garden Point. In 1990, the NT Historical Society published a book, *The Garden Point Mob*, in which former residents of the mission, now adults, described their lives with the nuns and their gratitude for that experience.

'Whenever I have mentioned to anyone that I was raised in a Catholic Orphanage on Melville Island, their first reaction is one of pity,' wrote one woman, 'but I soon put them into a clear picture of the wonderful childhood I'd had.'

Back in the 1950s, I had a poor opinion of government settlements like Warrabri and Papunya. To me they were show-pieces where scrubbed-up Aboriginals could be put on display. Given the slightest opportunity the Department would encourage distinguished visitors to the Territory to look over Papunya or Warrabri, and one often saw groups of well-dressed visitors, hands behind their backs (a la Prince Philip), promenading about these places, unclasping their hands only to take one more picture of the inmates as reminders of their visit to 'the Alice'.

In 1959, *Prospect*, a journal from Melbourne University, published an article I had written in which I described such settlements as 'human zoos'. I sought to point out that Aboriginals had been enticed to these settlements with visions of an easy lifestyle, only to be captured in an artificial and sheltered environment, and deprived of a purpose to life. These 'havens' fed their inmates processed food, gave them nothing to do, and gutted the spirituality and mythology and social life of the traditional culture. The end result was dehumanisation. Settlement Aboriginals were an undignified group of aimless, miserable and often ill individuals.

Today I might not be so judgmental. I am quite certain the workers in the settlements did their very best to make the settlement system work. Despite my criticisms then, I couldn't propose a better way to ease Aboriginals into our society.

A halfway house was essential, and so the settlements were probably as good as any other solution, although gathering many unsophisticated people together in one place accentuated the vices that were bound to appear. If there hadn't been a system holding back the thousands of natives that wanted to flock to the towns, Third World humpies and nightmare slums and exploitation by the white population would have been far worse.

Most people, black or white, wanted to do what they thought best, in accordance with their own code and culture. I used to think employment opportunities were the answer. Again, now I am uncertain. Throughout the 1960s and 1970s there was money and employment in abundance that could have helped Aboriginal communities in Victoria and NSW, yet despite the determination of the Whitlam Government, it came to little.

In the Territory I often heard it said that favourable treatment for Aboriginals (which we would now call positive discrimination) was bound to create and stir up ill-will, particularly from those non-Aboriginals who were competing for the same type of work, such as unskilled or semi-skilled labour. However real the history of anti-Aboriginal discrimination was, all the education in the world was unlikely to soften the hearts of those non-Aboriginals who were themselves doing it tough.

And what of the main players in my story? Well, Jerry Long is now retired from a very senior civil service position in Canberra and does some research and writing. I see him every year or so. He is a father and grandfather.

I caught up with Ted Egan late in 1996 at the launch of his excellent book *Justice All Their Own*. He also is a grandfather and well known as a singer, a man in love with the outback and a supporter of better conditions for the Aboriginals he loves.

Ted Evans never married and died in the early 1990s. He must be given an accolade for the stand he made in 1949. His forthright and, in public service terms, courageous act in bypassing his superior and reporting directly to the Administrator brought about huge changes in how part-coloured children were thereafter cared for.

Les Penhall is happy, healthy and enjoying his retirement in Darwin. Nosepeg, Ali Sawmill and Tuppa Tuppa are now deceased.

After leaving jail, Paul Ingram left the Territory. Once or twice in the 1960s I had a beer with him in

Melbourne. I believe he returned to Darwin and died a year or so ago. Ted Milliken, now in his mid-seventies, is still practising as a psychologist in Darwin.

For my part, I spent three idyllic years at Newman College at the University of Melbourne, finished law in 1961, then spent twenty-five years at the Melbourne Bar. I married and am now a grandfather.

In 1988, I was appointed to the Bench as Judge of the Accident Compensation Tribunal. That bench was abolished by statute in November 1992 in the political upheaval in Victoria that followed the election of the Kennett Liberal Government. Along with ten other judges I had my commission as a judge revoked. Fortunately, I was again appointed to the Bench, this time as a magistrate; probably making history as the only judge to end up so!

Some soporific summer afternoons on the Bench I jolt myself out of reminiscing of the Snake Bay beach, the endless tracks of the Kimberleys, Roger Jose, Olive Pink or whatever, and wonder if the barristers putting their arguments to me see me as some old bore as I once saw Sammy Dodds. Life – how the wheel turns!

Conclusion

I am often asked to comment upon contemporary Aboriginal affairs. My first reaction is to take the easy way out by stating the obvious, that I am way out of touch. Now that I have put this book together I would like to think that my story will help generate a better understanding of the 1950s assimilation policy of the Menzie's era, and an appreciation of Aboriginal culture.

Most people who discuss current problems associated with sacred sites and land rights – in my experience – do not show any real understanding of the fundamental nexus the traditional Aboriginals saw between themselves and their country. I have endeavoured in this book to show how basic and simple this nexus was and, in some cases, still is. In coming to grips with the problems of Aboriginal sacred sites, land rights and poverty, readers can better understand such matters by posing for themselves questions that may now appear appropriate to them.

Some people may denigrate Aboriginal claims by asking:

- How real can a belief in the traditional concept of procreation be today given our knowledge of biology?
- How real can it be for a person or group to say that their fertility depends upon an historic association with a particular geographical area due to that area having a Dreamtime significance?

But some others may argue that while an Aboriginal's strict adherence to a traditional belief may have waned in direct proportion to his or her acceptance of modern scientific reality, nevertheless an extraordinarily strong affinity to their country and that of their forefathers might still be quite understandable.

Those holding the latter viewpoint could argue that many professed Christians still see it as important to cling to the rituals of baptism or the eucharist. The underlying theology for baptism is the concept of original sin with its concomitant the afterlife state of limbo. How many who insist on baptism really believe in those concepts! For some Catholics the eucharist has its underlying theology bedded in the Thomistic and Aristotelian rationale of transubstantion; but I would bet pounds to peanuts a great many of the congregation and priests do not accept St Thomas's view. By the same token, why could not a modern Aboriginal have a very strong affinity and reverence for a 'sacred site' stemming from a respect for the memory and beliefs of his forbears, yet himself not believe in the essence of that Dreamtime story?

The High Court decisions in Mabo and Wik have stirred up the possum's nest no end, and properly so.

One of the principles distilled by these decisions is that prior to 26 January 1788 Australia was not a 'terra nullius' (no one's land), but rather a land populated by communities of peoples having a well-formulated law and culture. These communities were not ousted from possession of their land by conquest. Sadly, many of the original communities no longer exist, others exist in varying degrees of disarray, while some others such as the Tiwi and Pintubi continue to reside on their own lands. Surely justice dictates there must be communities that can claim title to the traditional country they still inhabit? The trouble is, as with many disputations, stating the principle of law is easy, but determining the facts finds one plodding through a quagmire of litigation and expense. As I have often heard and said in court, 'each case will be decided upon its own facts'. What more can I say upon the vexed question of land rights?

The sadness of the lost generation or the stolen children cannot be swept under the carpet. The experiences I have related in the book speak for themselves. Oh what a wonderful thing hindsight is! A 1930s Germany without Hitler! How could a whole civilisation let it happen? What about 'The Leaving of Liverpool'? Hundreds of children shipped out to Australia deluded into believing they were orphans and alone in the world. In my time in the law, children were taken from their parents as being 'likely to lapse into a life of vice and crime'. The list goes on.

When discussing this very sad problem, one must keep in mind the incredible stratification of society that existed in the Northern Territory. Imagine, if you like, the southern states of pre civil war United States. Give a Negro mother a choice of having her somewhat fairish child brought up segregated into black slavery or white freedom. Would she stand condemned for opting to give her child freedom and a vastly different future? Would he or she who helped that mother stand condemned? I am not for one minute justifying children being taken from a loving environment purely to 'turn a dirty little heathen into a nice clean Christian'. But there were cases when children were better off away from the environment of their birth place. Life as a citizen with the right to vote, to drink, and to be paid award wages, or life in the squalor of a stock camp, perhaps a flogging, little if any pay and to be the sexual toy of all who came by. The choice need not always be too difficult.

Much has changed. In the 1950s, in my experience, people of full Aboriginal descent rarely considered themselves as one with those of part Aboriginal background, and the reverse was also the case. When Des Morrison and I did the inspections along the Muranji track in 1957 we spoke to many part-coloured drovers who employed part-Aboriginal stockmen. A drover once said to me 'those blackfellas aren't really like us', and by 'us' he meant not other part-Aboriginal people but himself, Morrison and me.

Today the wheel has turned. Some people with the smallest claim to Aboriginal ancestry seem keen to abandon and deny all their non-Aboriginal forebears in order to be classified as Aboriginal, and rejoice in the community of 'our people'. It may be for the best of reasons but is certainly no time-honoured tradition.

Aboriginal policy has had many well-meant changes: 'smooth the dying pillow' of Daisy Bates, assimilation of the 1950s and 1960s welfare now. Perhaps all stages were necessary, but none have eradicated the evils of poverty and poor health. Ultimately, the Aboriginal people must be helped to stand on their own feet in a modern society without the need for any welfare other than is common in our community.

Appendix 1

25th August, 1959

TESTS TO BE APPLIED IN CONSIDERING WHETHER OR NOT A PART ABORIGINAL CHILD SHOULD BE TAKEN FROM AN ABORIGINAL MOTHER ON A SETTLEMENT OR PASTORAL PROPERTY

1. Acceptance or Rejection within the Native Camp
(a) If a male:
   Is he likely to be initiated in due course?
   Will he be allowed to take a wife according to tribal custom in due course?
   Is it possible that he may be expected to take a wife according to tribal custom, and if he remains to initiation with the tribe, would he be likely to offend members of the tribe or family if he refuses a full blood wife and prefers to marry a part aboriginal girl living under other than tribalised conditions?
   Is he fully accepted by his mother's husband, his mother's brother and his own brothers, as a member of the family unit, irrespective of his known non-aborigine paternity?

(b) If a female:

Was she promised at birth as the wife of some tribal male? If so, would it create any problems within the tribe if she were taken away?

Is it likely that, even if taken away for a time, she may subsequently return and accept the obligations of tribal marriage?

If she has not been promised, what is the reason? Could it be that her mother or mother's brother feel that she is not really part of the family unit? If so, do they tend to reject her in any way, or are they accepting (without perhaps verbalising it) that she will be taken from them in due course and placed in a children's home, thereafter to pursue a life other than that which is regarded as right and proper for full blood girls?

Is she accepted without question by other boys and girls as being properly part of the tribal group?

2. *Personal Outlook and Manner of Life*

Is the child, in habits and manner of life, identical with full blood children with whom he (or she) is living?

Does the child think of himself as being different in any way from his brothers and sisters or other children around? (It is rarely that a child consciously thinks that he is the same as other children – he would be aware of similarities or differences only on his awareness being awakened to differences.)

Are his pursuits, aspirations and general thought ways identical with those of other children around him?

Is there anything to suggest that the child, on reaching marriageable age, would find it more difficult than a full blood child to accept the responsibilities and conditions of tribal marriage?

In the case of a girl, is there any reason to feel that she would not accept, just as readily as a full blood girl, a tribal marriage in which she is one of a number of wives?

If a girl, does she know the man to whom she has been promised? If so, would she be likely to be mentally disturbed in any way by being removed from the tribal group and the locality?

In knowledge and habits, has the child a sophistication in sexual matters which could make him a problem in coming amongst European or part Aboriginal children, where, age for age, the same degree of sophistication does not exist?

3. *Educational Level*

At what level could a child expect to enter a European school, if transferred away?

If educationally retarded, and therefore in a class with younger children, has the child any other qualities such as sporting ability, etc., which could make him fully acceptable to children of his own age group, despite the fact that he is not with them in class during school hours?

What is likely to be the psychological affect of being in class with younger children, and possibly doing inferior work to many of them? Is there any chance that this could be offset by superiority in some other direction?

Does the institution to which the child is being transferred give any opportunity for him to display his prowess at skills such as tracking, spear throwing, etc., which may make him an interesting character to boys of his own age group, and thus mitigate the psychological ill effects of being placed in class with children who are his junior?

What is the child's ability to understand and to converse in English? If this is not great, what chance will he have of learning English before being plunged into the anxieties and uncertainties attendant upon removal to a completely new environment?

Where activities applying particularly to boys are mentioned, if the subject is a girl they should be replaced with equivalent activities appropriate to girls.

4. *The Parents' and the Child's Wishes*

Does the mother consider that removal is in the best interests of the child? If so, why does she think so?

Has the mother consulted either her brother or her husband on the matter of removal, and if so, is she acting independently of them, in agreement with them, or in opposition to their express wishes?

Does the mother wish to keep in contact with the child over the years?

Is the child prepared to make the break and launch out into a new adventure?

If the child is old enough to be consciously attached to his family group, but not old enough to comprehend the possibilities of the new adventure, in what way has the child been prepared for removal? What checks have been made to ascertain that the child is unlikely to suffer any permanent ill-affects, psychologically, from removal?

If there has been any reluctance on the part of the mother or child, on what grounds does the Removing Officer base his case for a continuation of pressure, on the parties concerned, to effect the removal?

5. The Attitude of Pastoral Management

What is the view of the Manager of the pastoral property regarding the removal?

If the child came back from an institution periodically, on holidays, would the pastoral management be prepared to accommodate him at the pastoral homestead and allow him access to his mother?

What are the characteristics of pastoral management's treatment of adolescent and adult part aboriginal persons living on the property?

6. Prospects of Employment

How would the child's prospects of employment be better after removal than they would be if left in the local environment?

In the case of a girl, has she better prospects of contracting a happy marriage ultimately, if removed, than she would have if she remained a member of her local community?

Would the child be at least as well off in the matter of employment, if left in his original environment, as he would be after removal from it, provided, in the first case, attention is paid to settling him in employment on reaching employable age.

7. Total Life Adjustment

Having considered all points separately, is the child likely to live a more contented, happy and fuller life, if removal occurs, than if he is left where he is?

Why could it be thought that the child's ultimate life adjustment will be more effective following removal than it would be without it?

What are the overall reasons in this case which make the Investigating Officer consider that removal is the best action to take in this particular case?

Appendix 2

20th November, 1957

ASSISTANT DIRECTOR OF WELFARE
(THROUGH THE ADMINISTRATIVE OFFICER (GENERAL))

PART COLOURED CHILDREN: WAVE HILL

1. Action regarding the placement of these children should be considered promptly if the best results are to be obtained.

2. Due to the various ages of the children and also their sex my recommendations for their future will vary.

3. At the time of my inspection of Wave Hill I found six part-coloured children whom I will consider individually below.

(a) <u>SHEILA</u>

    (i) Sheila, daughter of Elsie, aged nine years, file 56/1529 deals with the proposed adoption of this child. I do not recommend her adoption for two reasons. Firstly, she is almost ten years of age now, somewhat late I feel for a normal white family to admit her as one of their own children. Secondly, her social habit and behaviour is such that she is not even one step removed from the squalor of camp life as exists at Wave Hill.

(ii) I do recommend, however, that she be removed as I consider there may still be time to improve this girl's social status etc. Garden Point or Croker Island would be the immediate solution. Two years would be in my opinion the minimum time required to give Sheila a good working knowledge of our language and ways.

(iii) Finally, and this is common to all female part-coloureds, it has been noticed that girls a little older than Sheila become popular mistresses to both black and white persons in the outback, an argument greatly in favour of their removal to an institution.

(b) <u>PAULINE</u>

(i) Pauline, daughter of Elsie, aged eleven years. My recommendations in this case are similar to those made for Sheila. It is of importance however to mention that Pauline is already considered the tribal wife of one of the wards whose name for the present has slipped my mind. In view of this, Pauline is one of those border cases where it is difficult to judge whether or not removal is in the best interests for this girl's future and peace of mind. Nevertheless, if we could overcome the fact that she is tribally married, which I think we could, her age is such as to still give her time to throw off many of the influences of her past life, thus giving her the chance to take a fitting place in society.

(ii) Thus, as I said earlier, Pauline, like Sheila, should be removed to some suitable institution.

(c) JANE

(i) Jane, daughter of Elsie, is five years of age. Jane's age is such that if we could remove her from her present environment without too much suffering on the part of Jane or her mother, much good could be done, leading possibly to an adoption.

(ii) This then I recommend, that Jane should be removed to some suitable institution.

(d) JIMMY

(i) Jimmy, son of Tammerine, is five years of age. With the possibility of a school being opened at Wave Hill, I see no reason why Jimmy could not be educated there. Chaps of his position usually become good stockmen sometimes owning their own droving plants.

(ii) I think in the case of part-coloured males removal is not as imperative as in the case of females. However, if when the school eventuates, some lads show no desire for cattle work and perhaps aptitude for something else then I feel we should help them by widening their horizons.

(e) <u>BARRY</u>

(i) Barry, son of Tammerine, aged two years. Barry at two years or possibly three now could well be adopted. If this child had been a girl I would possibly recommend it. In this case I am hesitant, as I often wonder if the pain of separation is worth it in a lad's case. With distances being overcome and an increase in development within the Northern Territory, I feel that with the education he will get at Wave Hill he would make his own way in life, to take up a suitable station in life.

(ii) As such my recommendation is as for Jimmy (above).

(f) **JOCK**

(i) Jock, son of Daisy Chinaman, aged ten years.

(ii) My recommendation is that Jock be left where he is to serve as he is his apprenticeship in stockwork.

C. E. Macleod
Patrol Officer

INDEX

Aboriginal people
  and alcohol 2, 3–4, 27, 28, 43, 44–5, 46, 64, 65, 68, 69, 86, 142–3, 219–21
  assimilation policy 26, 71, 72–3, 75, 78, 83, 85, 87, 147, 166
  brutality against 38, 40–1, 45–6, 86, 155, 164, 165, 169–70, 172, 175
  camps 19, 28, 29–30, 37, 40, 85, 91–2, 147–8, 159, 160, 161, 164
  children 73, 82–4, 166–7, 170–6, 229, 239–49
  corroborees 60, 92–3, 126, 129–30
  culture 58–63, 64–9, 71, 72, 75, 79–81, 85–7, 92–3, 117–19, 136, 148–9, 159, 161, 180, 225, 233–4
  discrimination against 33, 35, 146, 154–5, 219–20, 221–4, 231
  Dreamtime 59–60, 87, 117, 148, 180, 219, 234
  education 82–3
  food 83–4, 86, 113–14, 131–2, 148, 159, 188
  health 82–3, 212–13, 224–5
  housing 19–20, 81–2, 85
  imprisonment 140
  labour 44, 121, 123, 133, 154–60, 162–3, 164, 169, 207, 228
  language groups 55, 80
  law 140, 207
  legislation 27–8, 50, 142, 163
  marriage 28, 57, 61–2, 65–6, 119
  part-coloured community 27, 35, 37, 43, 165–6, 167, 170–6, 239–49

relationship
- with Europeans 69–70, 149, 154–5, 172
- with police 45–6, 142, 219–20

religion 58, 60–1, 117, 118–120

sacred rituals 60–1, 118, 233–5

settlements, government 72, 78–80, 81–6, 107, 115, 120, 147–9, 177–8, 198, 228–30

sexuality 28, 58, 62, 65–6, 68–9, 118–19, 139, 207

skin groups 55, 56–8, 62, 87, 165

totem groups 58, 60, 61, 87

tribal
- disputes 57–8, 64, 80, 90–2, 139–40, 207
- groups 55, 58, 60, 61–2, 87
- lifestyles 55–63, 64–9, 71, 75, 79–81, 85–7, 116–19, 131–3, 136, 148–9, 161–2, 165, 170, 233–7

as Wards 2, 27–8, 49, 55, 80, 156, 165
- register 49–54, 55, 80, 141, 205

welfare 26–9, 43, 151–76

women
- abuse of 165–6, 171
- prostitution of 43, 46, 47–8, 65, 68, 69–70, 86, 142, 172

women's business 68

Agnes 78, 108, 109–10
Albrecht, Paul 2, 181, 205, 215
Ali Sawmill 112, 114, 126, 127, 129, 231
Allom, Doug 79, 83, 90
Allom, Mrs 82, 84, 128
Annie Yaws 70
Arthur, Joe 129, 130
Australian New Guinea Auxiliary Unit (ANGAU) 94
Australian School of Pacific Administration (ASOPA) 93–4, 96–100, 104

Bagot Settlement 37, 38, 66, 167, 209
Bates, Bill 216
Bathurst Island 107–16, 119, 134, 228
Battarbee, Rex 2
Bernard 120, 127, 133
Beswick Settlement 74–5, 79, 81–6, 87, 91, 108
Borroloola 197–9, 200, 205

Brennan, 'Tiger' 194
Bulldog 70
Bush, Brother 116

Calico Creek 110–11, 114, 125–6
Catarinich, Dr 7
cattle stations 73–4, 85, 154–5, 159–60, 162–3, 164, 207
Chooker Fowler 9
Church, the
 and removal of Aboriginal children 73, 166
Coburn, Bill 79, 83, 87, 179
Cosgrove, Father (Cossy) 116, 117, 134
Cousins, Mickey 168

Damaso, Babe 24, 34, 42–3
Darwin 19–21, 31–2, 34
Delissaville 134, 209–10
Dodds, Sammy 195
Driver, Mick 167
Dunn, Bill 217

Egan, Rae 197, 200, 203
Egan, Ted 24, 25, 26, 43, 46, 94, 197, 198–9, 231
Elkin, Professor A. P. 58, 94, 98, 147, 148, 222
Ellis, Tom 96, 101
Elsey Station 75

Emu Plains 110, 123
Eva Downs station 169–70
Evans, Ted 15, 18, 19, 23, 24, 25, 28, 34, 66, 139, 151, 152, 167, 168, 178, 183, 193, 194, 212, 231

Fisher, Tom 154, 161, 162

Giese, Harry 24, 25, 73, 127, 128, 129, 169, 172, 192
Gillsaeter, Mr 129, 130
Greenfield, Brian 94, 158
Groote Eylandt 139
Gsell, Monsignor 116, 118–19
Gunn, Aeneas 74

Harney, Bill 198, 210
Harold 145–6, 149, 150
Hasluck, Paul 27, 71, 104, 127
Haasts Bluff 177–9, 188, 190, 216, 219
Heath, Eileen 224
Henschke, Father 194–5
Hermannsberg mission 2, 177–8, 215
Hickey, Jack 124, 125
Hilda 78, 90, 108, 109–10
Hill, Ernestine 89–90
Hooker Creek Settlement 158, 165

Ingram, Paul 107, 109, 110, 125, 128, 129, 132–4, 135, 209, 210–11, 231
Ingram, Tessa 107, 108–9, 129, 209, 210

Jimmy Walrus 142
Jose, Roger 199, 201–4
Jumabaringa, Jimmy 38–9
Jumbo 66–8, 70

Kriewalt, Justice 41, 207

Lemaire, Jim 220, 222
Lennie 8
Leonard, Pat 94
Leydin, Reg 167
Lim, Charlie 31
Limundu, Dulcie 207
Litchfield property 66
Long, Gavin 26
Long, Jerry 24, 25, 26, 94, 177–8, 179, 182–3, 188, 231
Lovegrove, Creed 149
Lyons, 'Tiger' 194, 207

McAuley, James 98, 103
McCarthy, Brother 116
McCoy, Bill 214–15, 222
McKay, Jock 88–90, 107
McKay, Sandy 107–8, 109, 128–9

McKinnon, Macka 105
MacLeod, Ada 6, 16, 48
MacLeod, Alan 6
MacLeod, Jack 6
MacLeod, Ken 6, 16, 48
McNamara, Mary 191, 192, 194, 197, 209, 226
Mabo decision 234
Maddock, Jane 25
Maggie Dogface 46, 47, 72
Manly Surf Club 100
Mayall people 37
Mayne, Father 7
Melville Island 106, 107, 172–6, 228–9
Menzies government 27, 72, 233
Merlin, Mrs 24
Milliken, Ted 167, 169, 232
missions 2, 73–4, 107, 115–20, 166, 177–8, 215, 228–9
Morrison, Des 152, 153, 154, 156, 157, 236
Mukuljuk, Jack 67, 68
Mullholland, Jack 199
Murray, Jack 124, 135, 210

Namatjira, Albert 1–4, 219–21
Nicholls, Sir Doug 37
Nipper 78, 108, 110, 111
Northern Territory Welfare

Ordinance 27, 35–6, 43, 49–54, 68, 73, 91–2, 141, 151, 166, 172
Nosepeg 182–9, 219, 231

O'Brien Father 215
O'Keefe, Olive 224, 225
O'Loughlin, Bishop 22

Papunya settlement 177, 229
Penhall, Les 24, 25, 37, 38, 50, 142, 231
Pigface Polly 70
Pink, Olive Muriel 221–4
Pintubi 177, 178, 182–90, 235
Pitts, Alan 74, 76, 77–8, 79, 80, 82, 87, 88–9, 90–2, 209, 214
Point Lonsdale Surf Club 9, 100, 105
Pye, Brother 228

Rafferty, Chips 215–16
Rum Jungle 142
Ryan, Ron 74, 75, 77, 95, 154

Snake Bay 106, 107, 108, 110, 112, 126–7, 130, 228
Swanny 8

Sweeney, Gordon 28, 29–30, 36–7, 38–41, 42, 77, 170

Tiwi peoples 107, 112, 115, 117–18, 119, 120–1, 129, 136, 235
Tommy Oneleg 70
Tudawali, Robert 25
Tuppa Tuppa 182–7, 189, 190, 231

Warrabri Settlement 145, 147–9, 229
Wave Hill 151, 154, 157, 158, 161–2, 164, 167, 172–4, 245–9
Western Desert 178
Winnellie 19
White Australia Club 34
White Ensign Club 11
Whitlam government 230
Whitnall, Ron 194
Wik decision 234
Williamstown Naval Dockyard 5, 7–9
Williamstown Swimming Club 9

Yulungudi, Leo 207–8